THE ABODE OF
PEACE

Healing Your Life with
Gamma Energetics

EDUARDO PAZOS-TORRES

BALBOA.
PRESS

A DIVISION OF HAY HOUSE

Balboa Press books may be ordered through booksellers or by contacting:

Balboa Press
A Division of Hay House
1663 Liberty Drive
Bloomington, IN 47403
www.balboapress.com
1 (877) 407-4847

Print information available on the last page.

ISBN: 978-1-5043-9317-1 (sc)
ISBN: 978-1-5043-9319-5 (hc)
ISBN: 978-1-5043-9318-8 (e)

Library of Congress Control Number: 2017918440

Balboa Press rev. date: 01/29/2018

Contents

PART ONE

WHAT IS HEALING...3
    To heal is to recover natural happiness and pure love. 4
    Healing is to change to the highest mental and psychic level. ...6
    Healing is also establishing the equation of energy
    captured vs energy spent. 7
    Meditation is fundamental, as it is the most important
    activity of our life. 8
    Present, the infinite being and healing. 9

THE PILLARS OF TRUE SUCCESS 11
    Mind control. 12
    Exercise, meditation. 13
    Money and work 14
    Unconscious rejection of money. 16
    Pleasure, leisure, people, adventure....................................16
    Family..18
    Spiritual practice. 19

WHY GAMMA ENERGETICS? 22
    Freedom of beliefs. 24
    Quantum Mind. 25

PUT OUT THE TRASH 27

HAPPINESS CAN BE PERMANENT....................................29
    Learn to be happy. 30
    The reigning patterns. 32

The present now, the key to happiness. 34

FEAR, SILENT DISEASE 36
Fear is not yours exclusively. 37
The expression of fear. 38
Fear and external agents. 38
Fear and pain. 40
Fear and separation from divinity. 41
Fear and attachments. 43

THE PHOBIAS 46

INSTRUCTIONS ON HOW TO RELEASE FEARS 48

HOW TO DELETE REJECTIONS, HATES,
RANCORS, RAGE. 54

HOW TO ELIMINATE COMMOTION, ANXIETY
AND PANIC. 59

DEPRESSION 65

HOW TO RELEASE GUILT 69

HOW TO RELEASE ATTACHMENTS 75

EMOTIONAL PAIN, VIOLATION 81

HOW TO DELETE EMOTIONAL PAIN 85

PART TWO

BIO PHOTONS. 93
Empathy. 95
Quantum space. 95
The imagination. 96
Break the barrier of time. 97

THE THOUGHT-FORMS 100

THE LAWS OF THE UNIVERSE TO REPEAT ONE
EVERY DAY 102

ELIMINATE THE EGO OR SURRENDER 105
Letting in, letting go. 106
Reality is Change. 107
Do not resist. 108
Acceptance and Tolerance. 109
A war against everything and against all. 109
I am vulnerable, I am fragile, I am weak, I am defenseless.... 110
Beyond the Third dimension. 112
Everything matters nothing to me. 113

ELIMINATION OF MIND AND EGO WITH KRYON 114

HOW TO BE IN THE PRESENT- NOW 117

HOW TO BALANCE LIFE 123

SILENCE THE MIND FROM THE HEART 127

EXPERIENCE THE DIVINITY 134
The unlimited power of being (solitude). 135

MONEY AS ENERGY 139

THE PURITY AND DIVINESS OF SEX 147

PERCEIVE THE DIVINITY IN THE OTHER 151

I LOVE MYSELF 157

LIVING IN THE BEING 163
Select the Media. 164
Energy deficit and disease. 165
How to receive Prana. 167

ILLUMINATION 169

THE OASIS OF PEACE PYRAMID 174

PART ONE

WHAT IS HEALING

It is restoring the mind to its original level of peace and harmony. From the conscious it is difficult to identify the discrepancies that we have produced in it during the past that includes previous lives. When the unbalanced mind acts, its creations are full of pain and suffering.

The events of life create frictions and negative emotions that impact the body cells in their memory.

The functioning of the body is influenced by the mind and this in turn can distort the balance of the same. When I speak of mind, I mean not only the neural connections but also the linking of all body cells and the different focal points of the energetic anatomy of the electromagnetic field. An imbalance in the electromagnetic field caused by a foreign element like an entity or the trace of a psychic attack can also engender disease. Then the cleansing of the aura also gives us the balance needed to live happily.

Science has proven that the information of a human being, from the densest that is his physical body to the most subtle that is his spirit, is contained in only one of the trillions of cells that make up the human body. Therefore, healing must entirely encompass the cells of a person. Healing is to cleanse the remnants of unpleasant memories from experiences lived in this life or as a result of negative surpluses from other lives. It is to erase the painful and impure traces that impel us to act in an erroneous way in everyday life.

There is also an intimate connection between the physical body and the astral body, so that many healings and cures can be made more effectively at a distance. The astral body receives the information and moves it on to the mind where a misfit is formed which sometimes as a result it is somatized as a physical illness.

I call Healing the act of restoring balance in the conscious or unconscious mind of the individual. Healing is the cessation of physical illness as a result of a Health-giving process where the mind returns to act in harmony, peace and love.

Physical illness arises when the mind of the individual is full of negative feelings and emotions that drain the physical and mental energy. Emotions such as hatred, anger, resentment or rejection, produce conflict in the unconscious mind which in turn forces the body to produce hormones preparing it for combat. Hatred and similar feelings produce fear in the unconscious of the individual because in every war there are blows given and received, sometimes mortal. Many non-essential fears arise as a result of hate because we know that at any moment we can be attacked. In this same order of ideas, in healing animosities, rages and grudges we are freeing the mind of unconscious fears.

To heal is to recover natural happiness and pure love.

Healing occurs when the intimate relationship of the individual with his being or his own divinity is restored. What causes painful imbalance and suffering is the illusion of separation imparted by the senses. It is to only believe in the information of the senses. Information that changes, when we incorporate the sixth sense of

4

intuitive knowledge that we receive through the sixth Chakra or third eye and through the wisdom that is perceived in the fourth Chakra, also called the heart Chakra.

To Heal then, is to restore the divine powers of the human that have been incorporated as a divine spark or as a being in the image and likeness of God the creator of all that is.

Healing is to make another happy by sharing the energy of pure love that embraces all things. Healing is also transmitting happiness to another, restoring balance in his heart as to turn it away from the duality of pleasure- pain.

The delusion of separation keeps us in the dimension of pleasure and pain, in the illusory world we live in. This deception allows imbalance and disease to come through. When the human recovers his infinite being within, all kinds of diseases conclude and his life passes between happiness and satisfaction. Healing is to regain the innate happiness of being. It is to vibrate in infinite love and the desire to do what is good. It is retaking the energy inherent in all living things which links and communicates with everything through unparalleled joy that bursts out from their cells.

By erasing hate; a feeling contrary to the natural balance of pure and universal love; and expelling fears, guilt and depression, the authentic reality that we have lost for eons by giving preponderance to the ego and its illusory creations will shine forth. Elkhart Tolle, in his book 'The Power of Now', states that the true original sin is the supposed separation of the divinity that always resided within us, by the preponderance of the ego and the pleasures of the material world.

Life on earth offers a diverse experience of pleasures that should not be avoided. The error lies in attaching to and worshiping these pleasures and forgetting there is something deeper, immutable and eternal in the depths of our heart that communicates with the immanent happiness that is born but never perishes. Learning to always live in the infinite being is a guarantee for a life free from pain and suffering.

The philosopher stone on which Healing rests is to separate the ego and worship the inner divinity.

Healing is to change to the highest mental and psychic level.

By changing the instructions that reside in the cells, embedded as a result of previous events or experiences that created feelings, emotions or negative beliefs, we can recover the essential life of the cell that is based on universal love, and change the mental level of the individual. By cleaning external agents living in the aura as psychic attacks, curses, witchcraft, wandering entities and spirits, we restore the psychic natural balance of the individual and with it, the natural love that drives the cell to its maximum development.

Healing then occurs on the mental level and psychic plane of the individual as a mind that teaches another to live in pure love. Love is a universal condition that spreads through thought and psychic vibrations that lead to ideas, feelings and unitary emotions. Love spreads with thought and all humans who tune into its unique energy can enjoy it. Healing is restoring the union of the mind and psyche in universal love. This is one of the goals of this book: To propagate the frequency of pure and universal love to heal the planet and all beings that inhabit it.

Healing is also establishing the equation of energy captured vs energy spent.

When we're exhausted because of too much work or from investing time to suffer through scenarios and situations of terror that our mind elaborates, where the outcome is always negative and painful for us, it is easy for this mental monster to start working like a machine that debases and dominates us. The mind is not at our service. It is like a gadget of our invention that now enslaves us. We cannot free ourselves from mental compulsion. It is like an incessant train of thoughts that does not stop and brings anarchy to our life. We become prisoners of our own mind. Freedom then appears when we are liberated from this compulsive machine, when we are in the being, free from thoughts, feelings, emotions and negative beliefs.

We capture energy through food, the air we breathe, moderate exercise, *Chi Kung, Tai chi*, meditation and focusing on our infinite being with conscious breathing and remaining always in the now. Deep prayer and connection with our Master of Light is also another form of energy absorption. But how and in what do we spend that energy? Through everyday worries and obsession with painful outcomes in life's musings; In fear of experiencing one's existence; in anxiety for the changes that expel us from our comfort zone; in excessive work or living with someone who we do not tolerate; in fear of the future and its consequences in all areas of life; with the heavy burden of past emotions not erased from our unconscious; in the atmosphere of hatred that is perceived at work; with a boss and colleagues who steal our energy when we allow them; in watching or listening to news all the time that generate a state of anxiety and apprehension; in the attachments and fear of losing the object or person in which we center our painful love; in extreme ambitions that produce a state of permanent dissatisfaction; with greed and inability to obtain all the things we long for; in depression, sadness, anxiety, panic and all the emotions created by a compulsive mind, etc.

Every day we can develop new habits that allow us to recover lost energy. Meditation is beneficial, for just only 20 minutes a day. There are hundreds of meditation systems that help us focus energy. Some of these methods succeed in bringing the infinite being to the surface of the mind or at least manage to stop its incessant activity.

On the internet you can easily access *Falun Dafa*, a form of *Chi kung* which ends with a meditation that is complete because it captures *Chi*, both for the body and psyche through exercises and meditation that focuses all the energy received. I only recommend the exercises, not their philosophy. It is ideal for those who have little time.

Meditation is fundamental, as it is the most important activity of our life.

It is the intimate connection with the being. Transcendental meditation, *Kriya yoga*, or meditation with mantras, are schools that help focus energy. That being said, in my opinion the Melchizedech method is the best. After meditation you can listen to the recordings you have made on the different subjects you want to modify in your unconscious. Do not repeat the affirmations or instructions, which I will give later in this book, in your conscious because they do not have the same beneficial effect as on a deeper level just before finishing a meditation.

It is all about changing the emotions or beliefs through the brains right hemisphere (transcendent mind that reaches the unconscious) and not in the traditional way of reading that reaches the conscious but requires many repetitions. Whenever you feel a pernicious emotion, release it from your mind before entering into meditation and immediately listen to the instructions to eliminate that feeling, sentiment or belief. Another way is, at the end of each meditation, to have someone read you the instructions while you lie with your eyes closed.

In order to maintain a high energy level, in addition to the exercises that I teach with Gamma Energetics, you can read every day 'Practicing the Power of Now' from Elkhart Tolle, read excerpts from 'A Course in Miracles' or listen to the lectures of Pema Chodron. The important issue is to vibrate in universal love and to be aware of the inner infinite being. To be happy is always possible.

Gamma Energetics technique erases all negative feelings and emotions from the past residing in the cells; it eliminates all fears and concerns for an unknown future and prepares the mind to always live in the expression of the infinite being. In this way we guarantee an existence filled with happiness, achievement and creativity. A plethoric life of love and beauty. It is the healing that changes all the incongruities that pulsate in our bodies, for the satisfaction and joy of everyday life. It is the healing that connects us with our infinite being, with God the creator of all that is.

Present, the infinite being and healing.

Learning to be in the present-now free of pernicious memories that created drama in our life is another effective way to heal. Once we have applied Gamma Energetics to clean the distant past, recent past and even other lives, our mission is learning how to keep focused on the now. This is not an easy task considering the wild nature of the mind which cannot remain still for a single moment, wandering from thought to thought until it falls into a niche of pain and becomes obsessed. Here dread and inherent fear kidnaps the senses stimulating the imagination to create situations of terror that drain vital energy. The person feels devastated. The immune system yields to the pressure of the mind. The individual becomes aggressive, victim of obsession, not responding with gentleness to external stimuli because his organism is prepared for war. A baleful chain of reaction has been created which the individual is unaware of, being immersed in the succession of stormy events in his imagination.

To be in the present with the mind free of conversation is to enjoy the fullness of being, without worries concerning the future. It is to witness the astonishing beauty of a simple flower, to appreciate the magnificence of a sunset. It is enjoying our own breathing and delighting in the fascination for our own essence. It is to perceive the spell of people through their inner being. It is to perceive pure love in all that our senses concentrate on. It is relishing every activity as an innocent child, conscious of his games and hypnotized by his delightful occupation. It is to marvel at the majesty of life.

In practicing the inner silence for a few minutes, distracting the mind so it concentrates on breathing, from our spirit springs forth pure consciousness full of satisfaction and joy per se. Unpolluted love, happiness, harmony, tenderness and divine grace reside there, in the pure consciousness. It is a way of silencing the ego or the mind with its useless and perennial dialogue that deliberates between the divine and the human in an absurd and incoherent conversation.

THE PILLARS OF TRUE SUCCESS

To start with this topic, we will state that the most important thing is to sleep well. This means sleeping between 6 and 8 hours a day, according to each organism. We cannot speak of life quality without this fundamental requirement.

Restful sleep is the most formidable healing tool because it is like setting the body in automatic so that all non-volitional functions develop and eliminate the remnants of stress that daily activities and conflicts produce. So any healing technology must have a restorative rest response and vice versa, a deep sleep must help to heal all bodies, from physical to the quintessence of God.

Experts tell us that, in theory, we go through four phases of electrical brain waves emission. When awake, between 12 and 18 cycles per second of brain emission we are in *Beta* waves. We then move to *Alpha* waves for a period close to half -hour where the mind emits between 8 and 12 cycles per second, continuing to another 30 minutes cycle of *Theta* frequency (4-8 c / sec), then *Delta* (0.5 4c / sec), returning to *Theta*, *Alpha* and so on, the cycle continues. It is said that each cycle lasts an hour and a half.

It is recommended to sleep at least through 4 cycles or being in the arms of Morpheus during 5 cycles, plus a half - hour interregnum; that is, a total of 8 hours for an intense and effective energy repair.

Mind control.

Maintaining healthy thoughts are also a priority when looking for a balanced daily life. Being aware of the repair process is a simple exercise to keep the mind trained, away from harmful thoughts, feelings or emotions. Living in the present-now enables us to abandon vicious circles of torturous thoughts and suffering.

To focus energy during activity, focus your attention on breathing, on the action of inhaling and exhaling. This simple trick takes out thoughts full of fear, hatred and envy. Always strive for awareness to be in the present-now because it is the simplest way to enjoy life's elemental pleasures and to savor the sweet sensations of the infinite being within. This enjoyment is unparalleled. Feel from the present how everything around you is energized.

Learn that in order to be happy you only need to contact your infinite being, independent of being accompanied, living extreme luxuries or possessing things and power over others. Happiness is a free gift that life gives us, packaged in the heart of all human chakra. It only takes will and knowledge to be in the ineffable company of the infinite being.

This is In fact one of the goals of incarnation: to discover the indescribable goodness of the inner being. It is a gift that we have all received but most of us ignore. To be aware of the infinite being means to live paradise in this life, independent of poverty or wealth. That is why the ancient Vedas said that this life is an illusion because the only thing that is immutable is the being; and all material things, the body, people, circumstances and facts are subject to permanent change. Do not live clinging to your wealth or poverty because the essence of life is change. If you concentrate on living your infinite being, you will be drinking the elixir of eternal life, because life is to be born and to die, but our being is eternal.

Ancient alchemists intended to turn all the elements into gold. The true alchemy of life is to turn all tortuous and painful thoughts into spiritual pleasure of the infinite being. To live in the self is the highest glory a human can experience. Having the infinite being inside turns all suffering and drama into the most harmonious and enjoyable life experience beyond the roller coaster of pleasure and pain.

Exercise, meditation.

For a balanced mind, body and spirit, monitor the quality of your thoughts. To achieve this, maintain a daily routine of meditation, to focus the mind, and physical exercises to oxygenate and rejuvenate the body. *Chi Kung, Falun Dafa, Taichi, Yoga,* Jogging, non-competitive sports and walks in nature all contribute to revitalize the body and energize the mind to face the challenges of existence.

There are hundreds of styles of meditation according to the likes of each person. Meditation helps to connect with the inner being, center the thoughts from their natural chaos, organizes the mind, clarifies the analysis and maintains a level of peacefulness in any situation. In this order of ideas it is of key importance to eliminate hatred because it is the most harmful emotion there is. In the same way, learn with Gamma Energetics how to exorcise your fears and be able to launch yourself to enjoy the adventure of life with new challenges.

Exercise should be moderate. Its main goal is to keep the body healthy, the cells oxygenated, to preserve vitality and feel physical fullness. Spending large amounts of energy in a short time-period is a sure way to deplete reserves. In the energy-input-output equation, let us try to keep a surplus for a healthy balance. If we spend more energy than we gain with food, meditation and sleep, we are paving the way for disease.

Being surrounded by nature ensures that we capture the surplus Prana force of trees without doing exercise, in what the Japanese call "forest bath". Try to practice techniques that fill you with energy over those that wear it out.

Consider as a challenge or adventure those obstacles that arise as they will allow you to feel adrenaline and then enjoy the sensation of physical and emotional pleasure when the turbulence has passed. Comply with everything that happens and do not fight stubbornly so that results are given as you want. Most of the time the outcome is better than expected, but if not, accept it without resistance. Be like flexible bamboo in the wind, which withstands all the storms while other trees that oppose resistance, are uprooted.

Money and work

Work is one of our main concerns. It is the activity where we spend most of the time. Our physical and mental health depend heavily on the nature and quantity of it. It is necessary to love what we do and in the best of scenarios, do what we love. If there is no love for work, we are faced with the germ of disease. It is preferable to change activity for something that we fully enjoy. Productivity standards skyrocket if we are hooked on the work we like and bring us satisfaction. We can be busy for many hours and not feel tired. In all cases it is wise to work up to a maximum of 8 hours per day because exceeding the natural wear of the body and nervous system leads to illness. On the other hand, taking a vacation and disconnecting from work problems are priorities; for this we must meditate and emphasize sports or artistic practices that will separate us from labor routine. In addition, the excess of work leads to a decreasing marginal performance, that is, the quality of our work is reduced substantially, when we exceed the limit of 8 hours.

A common way to drain or expend energy is to have a bad relationship with the people we work with. It is an invisible and sometimes imperceptible war.

We are prepared to attack or feel victimized. The prevailing feelings are anger, rage, envy, hatred, resentment or revenge. When war unfolds, the consequences are disastrous. Through the procedures of Gamma Energetics we must heal those feelings and negative emotions to get a healthy working environment. By law of resonance, the person subject of those feelings changes in a positive way with us when we eliminate these negative feelings from our mind. The world and its evolution are equal but if we substitute the perception we have of this person for one full of kindness and eliminate resistance and accept events as they come, we then change our karma. Being noble in character saves us a host of problems. Clearing our negative emotions increases the possibility of worthy interpersonal relationships.

At work there are many negative beliefs reflected in people because there is a constant exchange of information between human beings. Denying the principle of authority, rebellions, hoarding the tasks of others with disastrous results, avoiding responsibility or heaping work on an efficient person, are failure examples of programs inserted in people's minds throughout their life and that deserve to be healed forever. We all carry the burden of negative or positive emotions to the outside world. Within relations at work we find that many employees continuously get sick while having a demanding and unfair boss. The trending human talent development techniques involve exercises to make the worker feel happy in his environment and thus increase productivity. Leaders are the first ones who qualify for healing because if at the top of the organizational structure there are neurotic persons in charge, the whole pyramid is infected by bad relationships, war and suffering.

Unconscious rejection of money.

By a culture factor of this or other lives some people regard money as something vain and sinful. In fact, in the church many mantras are heard against money. Modify your stance against wealth or money and do not reject it. Having money is not a sin and does not rule out the possibility of it contributing to your welfare. Neither will you be vetoed to enter into the kingdom of heaven. In fact, if we learn to live, the kingdom of heaven can be there in your heart, in the infinite wisdom of your being. Certain paradigms like 'a rich man will not enter the kingdom of heaven' have been used to destroy the legitimate ambition of man to conquer wealth with intelligence and work. A different thing is the greed in which 'the end justifies the means' and therefore all sorts of arbitrariness and evil are committed in order to get rich. But in a legitimate way, every man has the right to abundance and wealth. Use the Gamma Energetics toolbox to erase all your guilt and demonization programs from your psyche.

Work aimed at serving humanity produces the highest satisfactions and varied forms of wealth. Arising in the morning with the mind concentrated in solidarity and compassion for others generates indescribable happiness. A clear mind product of being clean of thoughts, feelings, emotions or negative beliefs, makes the path ready for a plethora of successes and satisfactions, an enjoyment in every moment for the simple reason of being alive. It is implicit joy as if we were connected to a great center of divine energy. Events become secondary as we prevail in the pure love that emanates from our center-heart.

Pleasure, leisure, people, adventure.

We live in an epicurean age of being bound to the pleasure of the body and senses. Some of these pleasures later become disease and torture for humans. Like all excess, the threshold of pleasure fades to become an executioner. If we learn to live in the now, in the wonderful sense of openness, of peace that is born in the heart-chakra, our life will be something else. All worldly pleasures are valid because we are in the interior of a physical body. But bondage to pleasure and excess creates pain when the source of fruition disappears or when the limit of ecstasy is reached and depression ensues. Some heroic drugs and alcohol squander our reserves of brain hormones and consequently we feel depressed, melancholic, sad and dejected.

Finding inner peace in the center of our spiritual heart gives us the balance to enjoy every second of existence, because true happiness does not come from things or people but from the infinite being within. A sense of joy and serenity lies at all times just by being aware of our connection with the divine, through meditation or communication with a divine being through prayer.

Contact with nature through forests, parks or the ocean are means for recharging our body batteries by capturing the Prana that emanates from these sources. The forest bath is an activity that gains more and more followers. The company of pets or affectionately observing animals is another important resource in the absorption of the Prana of life.

Learning to live teaches us balance. Exercising, food, sex, hobbies, travel and contact with nature are key in taking a break from problems that a world of savage capitalism proposes. But enjoyment without excess, in the right measure, is the golden rule for relaxation and recharging the body with Prana or vital energy.

When we talk about leisure we mean those recreational activities in which the individual feels free. It is the 'Dolce Far Niente', the pleasant relaxation in carefree idleness, where the infinite being arises within. It may be meditation, awareness focused on the mere act of breathing, development of an action that provides soul pleasure, the practice of our favorite sport or delighting in a creative or artistic work. In all these tasks the common denominator is the uptake of *Chi* or Prana to fill the energy storehouse of body and psyche.

Friendship with other human beings is the most important link in our lives. Science has proven that our brain produces oxytocin, dopamine, phenylalanine and endorphin, hormones responsible for building wellness, joy and enthusiasm while reducing the stress in the individual who enjoys the company of his friends. Friends give comfort in difficult times and share the pleasant experiences of life. Cultivating friends is a guarantee for mental health.

Family.

Family is another very important sphere of our existence. We work and struggle to share our income with our loved ones. The family is the essential nucleus in balancing the individual. Maintaining coherence and family unity should be one of the precepts in daily life. Disease can occur if we neglect this primordial aspect. The family is synonymous with solidarity, company and integration. It is the escape valve from events that strike us. The family is the loving sustenance of mankind. The energy that emanates from its members is the most powerful booster of love, courage, optimism and understanding that encourages us to continue this journey called life.

Enjoying our family as much as possible every year of our existence is the irreplaceable engine of human productivity when love and compassion reign among its members.

If we neglect any of the premises mentioned above, we cannot say we are successful. Our passage through this existential world must maintain a balance between work, duties, pleasure, friendships and family. Here it is worth emphasizing the importance of eliminating attachments in order to enjoy ourselves without pain. To be able to love people, activities or things without the pain that produces its loss. In the Gamma Energetics toolbox, there are several techniques to eliminate attachments and emotional commotion by the loss of people or objects we love.

Spiritual practice.

During the activity we can be aware of our breathing and contact our divine interior. In speaking of a spiritual practice we emphasize having time to be aware that our identity is not the body we inhabit. In other words, spiritual practice is to spend time to feel the true essence of being. A person who is too busy does not have time to enjoy the love of his family and even less to enjoy the ineffable pleasure of the inner being. That is why we stress the importance of meditating to unite in communion with the infinite being. It is vital to destine time to feel the divine presence as the most important daily activity that we can perform to nourish the soul, as well as food and restful-sleep to feed the body. In fact, when someone is permanently connected to his being, he does not need food from nature to subsist, as he is only nourished by Prana or vital energy that he captures through breathing.

There are records of thousands of people who do not need solid food to survive. The Australian teacher Jasmuheen, a Breatharian, instructs through her theory how to obtain food for the body from breathing. The core of her method lies in being aware of the infinite being within each one and breathing towards that universal energy center. When spiritual practice is repeated daily or in every moment free of daily actions, it becomes the axis of our life and a connection with the immanent happiness that arises from being.

Of all commitments this one is the most important, by which we reincarnate and support the fulfillment of the mission to purify our soul in this body. Everything else is adjective and secondary. Spiritual evolution involves the end of mysticism focused on external forces and teachers outside of man to grant the real value of the human in the history of species. This evolution is a recognition of the divinity that rests in each individual who has transcended its ego. This does not mean to break with the beliefs that have been massified as religions for the last 5,000 years, but to transcend them. It is about turning the attention to the interior of the human being to find the answers and not to perpetuate the search in the external to explain its divine nature. Great teachers interpreted for the good of humanity, not their haruspices. It is the end of the story for spiritual intermediaries called pastors, priests or ayatollahs and other hierarchies.

Communication with the divine source is individual and non-transferable, exempt from tolls of any nature. It is the elimination of the influence of sacred texts and their interpreters in the pacification and harmonization of the human by the individual search of its own divine essence. Every human being seeks for an end to his ego as the main obstacle to procure his own happiness and fulfillment. The less developed consciences will be replaced in the driving sphere of the countries and the planet to redirect humanity towards an authentic destiny of overcoming as a species. If leaders have had psychopathy and mental illness as a common denominator, there will now emerge real spiritual heights in the conduct of humanity. It is the prioritization of the search for truth and of human spiritual conquest as a divine creature of the most perfect bill. It means a change in production structures and equal distribution of wealth so that we all fit in this world in similar conditions and love and compassion for one-self arise, which is the basis of love for others.

Spiritual work is to break down all barriers so that the divine being shines within each one and the Olympus ambrosia reigns in our hearts. It is to be connected day by day, moment by moment, with divinity's pure dimension and anchor there the course of life as a joyful story. It is to retain the subtle power of universal love to irrigate it in all consciences. It is living nirvana in a way never dreamed of, in our existence here on earth and in unity with all beings.

WHY GAMMA ENERGETICS?

The goal of this healing technology is to find the divinity present in all human beings. When the mind is in the now, it enjoys unity in pure love in the 5th dimension with all that is. It is through love that the human can perform the greatest feats and even command on organic and inorganic matter. It is the natural way in which great avatars produce miracles because they live in that divine frequency of pure love.

The purpose of this book is to guide each one in the how- to-obtain the vibration and frequency of the present-now by means of meditations that command the trillions of cells of the human organism to enjoy the delights of living in that dimension. When we become centered in the now, the all-connecting inner divinity and unparalleled bliss invades all our bodies: physical, astral, pranic, emotional, mental, karmic and spiritual.

In order to complete this task with optimum results, we approach the cleansing of low frequency emotions from the past and future, feelings and beliefs that govern the individual's unconscious and incite him to act wrongly in the course of life. This erroneous act is a great detonator of pain and suffering.

According to the convention accepted as a pattern of measurement, our mind adopts different frequencies according to the states of consciousness or unconsciousness that it lives. Thus it can pass from Beta state or awake, to deeper states like Theta or Delta during sleep or hypnosis and in some exceptional cases, to be in the Gamma frequency when the brain emits more than 40 cycles per second; a state in which the mind is awake but at the same time in the enjoyment of the wonderful ambrosia of pure love.

The great masters of the Indian, Chinese and Japanese cultures teach us different types of meditation, whose primary objective is to contact and awaken in each human being that divine spark of which Jesus Christ spoke. That divine touch is indeed latent in every human and we can bring it into an active state in order to live paradise on earth. It is what we call awakening and enlightenment. In very deep states of ecstasy through meditation, the brain emits more than 40 cycles per second which is the so-called Gamma frequency; in this vibration we feel compassion for what exists and we unite in universal love to everything. Through this technology named Gamma Energetics, we achieve to lead the reader or client to the frontier of enlightenment and his evolution depends on the karmic factors of each individual so that that quantum leap is crystallized in this life. But in the interregnum, Gamma Energetics gives each person who practices it, moments or hours of indescribable happiness above the conditioning of daily routines by transforming pain and suffering into joy and profound bliss.

With Gamma Energetics, there is no need for you to retreat to the mountains to isolate from mundane noise. The incredible fruition and delight that comes from your heart will be easily accessible where you are every day, as you practice these exercises and heal your mind of low frequency energies. At the same time, Gamma Energetics gives you the tools to heal others and induce into your infinite being an ocean of joy and happiness.

Freedom of beliefs.

This methodology of work respects the beliefs and ideologies of each one but emphasizes that the communication with the divine energy is feasible in each and every human being without any type of intermediation. In other words, the divine source of all that is or God resides in each one of us as Jesus and other avatars affirmed. The vital energy that creates and modifies everything resides in the atom as well as in the cosmos. It expresses itself as ineffable and indescribable love that arises in our heart-chakra and pervades the trillions of cells in our body.

We achieve this state of consciousness by suppressing the mind and the ego for a time so that it radiates the inner divinity with its own light. Turning off the mind is one of the purposes of this work; to ignite the divine spark in the center-heart and enjoy the capture of Prana. The possibility of healing others with quantum physics (an issue that we will address in other books) and to live the fullness of life with satisfaction and delight is the other objective.

Our body is a holographic sample of the universe which we inhabit and our center-heart is a fractal of divine energy that creates and modifies everything.

It is not necessary today to live in a monastery to obtain the divine Amita. The gamma energy emissions of the sun and the central star of the galaxy are modifying our DNA in such a way that to learn and evolve we can escape suffering and pain.

Gamma Energetics is a powerful healing technology; Easy to implement and with quick and surprising results. It is the outcome of multiple teachings of traditional teachers and modern channels of more developed cultures.

Quantum Mind.

According to Max Planck's theory, the originator of quantum theory, the universe is influenced by consciousness through the mind. If we cleanse the mind from negative thoughts and emotions of the past and projections into the future, our brain will be very powerful to connect with that consciousness and modify the world according to our desires. Of course these must be accompanied by the most powerful of all forces: Pure love.

The words we utter translate as vibrations and frequencies in the mind with which we resonate. We construct our reality by a quantum law in which like attracts the like. This truth acts in our body with the production of enzymes and hormones that turn our thoughts into action. If they are of love, we overflow the body with dopamine, oxytocin and serotonin that provide maximum well-being in all organs and systems. If on the contrary the thoughts and emotions are of hate or fear, a harmful chemical reaction runs through the body, segregating adrenaline and impelling the person to become aggressive, due to the negative thoughts he has driven and diminishes the ability of the immune system to defend the body from diseases. This is one good reason to harbor and produce positive thoughts throughout life. The chemistry of words engenders discomfort or well-being in the rational individual's body and creates a wave of photons that alter the environment around them.

The goal of Gamma Energetics is to modify the programming of the body cells to clear negative thoughts, feelings, emotions and beliefs and to turn our cellular store into an emporium of virtues, peace, happiness and love for all the beings of this world, as well as to cultivate a promising present and future.

Another key subject of Gamma Energetics is addressing the heart-chakra as the central focus for exercises that stimulate the chemistry of love. In the center-heart, or fourth Chakra, we hold a force of incredible vigor that we call the infinite being.

When we are in tune with the infinite being, a wave of magic, beatitude and compassion surrounds everything around us. It is spiritual alchemy that turns any fact or thought into universal love by passing it through the center-heart filter.

In short, we get to be in the present-now and enjoy the ineffable happiness of being in the center of our chest, without ego or mind in liberation from the pleasure-pain duality.

Life will present its difficulties but we will face them with other mental patterns that bring us out of the chains of thought that lead to pain or suffering. We will receive all gifts of daily life with gratitude and with the exalted qualities of the soul that arise from the center-heart to share as a beautiful present with others, without resistance, as events, with a very high vibration and the most refined feelings.

According to Seth, consciousness is like a lamp that we can focus in different directions around us. We are accustomed to a single focus where our ego resides. If we turn the lamp we will become aware of our multidimensional being independent of the ego as the center. In these exercises we seek to focus the mind on our emotional, mental and spiritual bodies to produce fundamental changes in the unconscious and heal pain, sadness and depression. We always have the option of changing the channel of consciousness to live in the eternal happiness of being. We can focus on healing our cells from other lives, on genetic inheritance, on the ancestral curve and thus producing the longed for harmony, peace and happiness of our being in the fifth dimension.

PUT OUT THE TRASH

Imagine a house where for 20 years or more the trash has not been removed. Microorganisms build their empire and create their breeding ground for disease. To live among that rottenness becomes an epic task. Being happy is almost impossible because of the amount of dirt that invades us which in practice does not allow us to mobilize. Then comes the repugnance for the filth that has seized our dwelling. This happens when we have never cleansed the psychic world of the mind and its phases of consciousness and unconsciousness.

We have all heard of the importance of forgiveness, not so much to ingratiate ourselves with others as to alleviate our own tension. Well, most people wander the streets and sidewalks of this planet without knowing that hatred, rejection, anger, rancor, anxiety, panic, fears, phobias, attachments, commotion, depression, guilt, etc., must be first removed from their mind to preserve mental, emotional and physical health. True happiness of the individual occurs when these emotions have been erased and mind's true nature emerges and connects with everything in a symphony of ineluctable love. It is the presence of being, rescued from the bowels of pain and pleasure. Man is born HAPPY per se, independent of things, people or circumstances that surround him, but then there arises in him the seed of discord that condemns him to live the roller coaster of pleasure and earthly pain. When man is freed from this yoke of feelings, emotions and beliefs, he experiences heaven on earth; the eternal emotion of universal love that permeates everything and the peace that adorns a splendid life of service to other humans.

This book teaches you how to take the psychological garbage out of your cells and walk lightly to face the challenges of existence, regardless of the religious ideas you profess or life's blows, and to always be happy and calm. Needless to say, if we have an emotional balance we can cure the diseases that once afflicted us and in the future world, to prevent other ailments that could arise, because healing penetrates the higher world of consciousness where energy is expressed.

Another consequence of healing negative emotions is rejuvenation. Body cells change all (including neurons) in a period of up to 2 years. Aging is a silent disease induced by unhealed painful feelings or strong emotions that coexist in the cells of an individual. When a person heals hatred or trauma that accompanied him for a period of time, his rejuvenation can be noticed by a relaxation of the tense body that held that psychological garbage. After cleaning up a negative emotion look at yourself in the mirror and you will notice how you have recovered freshness and youthfulness.

HAPPINESS CAN BE PERMANENT

Everything has to do with evolution of our personality through the lives we have lived and the subsequent lives we will live. Healing is not only feeling better, but also stable and stronger in the physical level, to enjoy all the minimal experiences of this existence. It also prepares, if necessary, the ground for our next incarnation to fully and consciously enjoy the varied scene of physical, emotional and psychic satisfactions.

Our thinking is like a lighthouse that is guiding the roads which we will travel in this vital journey. As we think, we are. In what way we think, in that way we will build our destiny. For this purpose we rely on our mental and psychic abilities that translate into skills used to obtain the accomplishments that each one draws as a goal.

The main object in the daily occurrence is to respect all consciences that coexist with us on the planet. All consciousness is sacred. Otherwise we all execute ourselves by not considering nature and its conservation cycles.

An erroneous understanding of the human race is that databases which exist in the conscience or in the psyche of any individual are fixed and unchangeable. Today we know, because science has proven so, that the cells of a human can be reprogrammed to improve it in all aspects of life, from physical to spiritual.

Deprogramming of pernicious or harmful habits that are modified by more efficient or healthy ones develops in a simple way, because the cells obey thought or word in certain states of consciousness. In this way, any individual can become more intelligent, assertive, productive, efficient and even more satisfied and happy than before undergoing changes in his mind and psyche.

Learn to be happy.

Fill the present moment with images that bring you peace, happiness and self-realization.

Have an arsenal of pleasant memories or beautiful images, to reminisce emotions and feelings of joy. Always tune into channels of consciousness with information that produces fulfillment and happiness.

Review a photo album of places you have visited where you have been happy and satisfied.

Review happy moments with someone in different circumstances.

Listen to a symphony or a musical piece and concentrate only on living each beat and each instrument.

Listen to music that makes you feel cheerful and happy.

Caressing a loved one and reminiscing magical moments with that person.

Pamper a pet.

Revive intense moments of full realization in the company of nature.

Bring to mind the graduation moments from high or professional school.

Remember moments when you were praised in public.

Look back to that intense emotion, when your children or relatives were awarded.

Recall beautiful moments with your family.

Remember funny situations where you laughed out loud.

Watch a comedy and laugh whole-heartedly.

Go to a play and feel each of the characters.

Go to a concert of your favorite artist.

Revive a concert shared with friends.

Live with all intensity the highest moments in a spiritual ceremony, a temple or a church.

Recall the peak moments when your soul has reached unspeakable dimensions of rapture and spiritual pleasure.

Read jokes.

Recall a meal or banquet where your senses were full of pleasure and

completeness.

Look back to those stellar moments when you felt inside the divinity of being.

Experience the supreme happiness and joy that reside in your heart chakra.

Be cheerful, uncomplicated, and happy.

Perceive the confidence and fullness of the infinite being within.

Remember with luxury of details a trip to nature.

Go to the countryside or to a park to contemplate its greatness and each one of the beings that inhabit there: trees, trunks, flowers, leaves, insects, until you feel the divine connection with them. Remember extraordinary landscapes and feel how you get involved in that experience as to feel it in your skin; smell and breathe that beautiful place.

The reigning patterns.

First let us change all the harmful or destructive habits that invite us to fail in obtaining a more pleasant existence. This is our guarantee for changing whatever prevents us from progressing or being happy right now. In this range we will consider all the vices or addictions that make life unbearable and make us avoid actions that we consider beneficial in daily life. Here it is crucial to eliminate all kinds of attachments and to erase the implicit suffering or pain that comes with them.

The next modifiable point is fear that traps us and excites the imagination so that our goals become distant or improbable. Nothing else limits our freedom as much as these negative emotions embedded in the unconscious of the psyche. If something paralyzes action is the negative influence of fear for the unknown or of the future that we construct day by day. Acting helps us demonstrate that most fears are unjustified and belong to the useless and permanent dialogue of our conscious mind. Leaving the comfort zone is a challenge for someone who wants to give a little adrenaline to the incessant routine. For this, going ahead of fears is imperative. But it is not so complicated if we apply the Gamma Energetics technology to reprogram the subconscious mind in that matter.

Other feelings that poison the mind and therefore the body are anger, rejection, rancor, rage and hatred. In cleaning the past, any aftereffects of these feelings must be erased from cellular memory. Nothing engages us as much as hatred for someone or something so that we share it for so many lives until we release it. Nothing hurts us more than hating. It is the antipode of universal love that brings us so many benefits. Hate or envy prepares the body for permanent war until we deplete our adrenaline reserves and our body organs and systems succumb to terminal illnesses. We must erase from the consciousness of each atom of our personality these feelings, emotions or thoughts that stimulate an absurd war with other humans, things or animals. Hatred kills without mercy the unfortunate owner of this feeling. By cleansing it we release our cells to bring optimism and joy implicit in daily living.

Guilt is another foundation on which our civilization is based on. It is a tool for slavery frequently used in all media to subject others. Guilt, sin, and error make the person deserving of punishment. Guilt and sin inhibit the full functioning of the mind to create a better world for us. The merit for punishment implicit in guilt generates the greater volume of illnesses that the individual attracts to pay for his mistakes. If Newton's third law tells us that every action produces a reaction, why speak of guilt and sin? If everything that each individual produces as a result of his action generates a contrary reaction, what object is there in blaming or calling the subject sinful? Is it not an additional or psychological punishment for those who act in this way? Guilt and sin invite us to be manipulated by those who claim to be the representatives of the divinity on earth. In this way we deny our divine essence and intimate connection with the divine.

Guilt causes the greatest number of diseases in the individual who unconsciously claims to be punished for his actions. This punishment is psychosomatically self-inflicted and results in diseases that are difficult to diagnose by regular medicine.

When law is broken by the individual, he receives his sentence or punishment. If laws of this world do not punish him, the laws of the universe take care of doing so in this life or another to comply with Newton's law of energy. Then it does not make sense to call the ordinary human a sinner, nor to impose additional guilt on him. In fact, when we call another a sinner, we establish a difference between ourselves, a distance that repels us from loving our fellow men without measure. When we feel as sinners, we implicitly ask for additional punishment that already life gives us in its wisdom and we block our desires and dreams believing we do not deserve them.

Another emotion or feeling of great impact is the sensitive pain or trauma produced by specific situations of violence or fear in a person's life. By erasing these impressions from the cell we release organs and sometimes complete systems in the physical body. We face one of the biggest generators of panic and fear. Once we learn the lesson this situation left as an experience it is easy to eliminate it from the individual's history. By cleansing the trauma, all bodies experience peace and liberation that allows them to reach a level of happiness by the simple fact of existing. But releasing the unconscious from a tortuous past is not enough to attain full happiness. It is required to teach the cells to live in the present.

The present now, the key to happiness.

By cleansing the reigning patterns that bind us to the past and changing them for healthier ones, we take a step forward in our evolution. But not everything is finished. This imminent change of our cells in the liberating past allows us to stay away from the obsession with some past circumstance and is an indispensable tool in finding mental balance. Now we have the challenge of changing the mental patterns of time which we have learned for eons and that keep us clinging to suffering and existential pain.

FEAR, SILENT DISEASE

In this century of Internet and immediacy, fear is projected as a plague that scourges the whole of humanity. If you analyze the content of television you will find that news is written by journalists full of fear who wish to sow collective panic, even if it is not a deliberate act. Advertising is developed to cover the fear of sickness, death, old age, or economic insolvency. Other products are sold to alleviate the fear of malnutrition, ugliness, obesity or skinniness. The fear of loneliness is implicit in the advertising of plastic surgeries and gyms.

Fear of communist or fascist totalitarianism is promoted in political advertising. In the latter, people are persuaded to solve hunger, misery, malnutrition, illiteracy, homelessness and fear of disease through health systems.

Peace or fear of war is explicit in many political campaigns as a decoy to attract voters. Churches promote fear of hell and demonization of other beliefs to avoid the migration of their faithful clients. The fear of divine punishment leads millions of people to pay their tithes as taxes to gain a place in the glory of God.

There are thousands of fears, from losing a school or university year to losing our job, partner, or the reality of death that surrounds our lives. Insurance advertising is led directly to dreads of fire, assaults, earthquakes, accidents, old age and death.

Fear is not yours exclusively.

We are all networked, as Gregg Braden, American scientific and metaphysical physicist, has shown in the holographic matrix. This means that Homo sapiens is connected in an interdimensional way with all beings and influences the process of transformation of the nature of cosmos and individuals themselves.

In addition to the propagation of fears through all modern forms of communication or media, our own electro-magnetic essence-light allows us to receive and transmit thoughts, feelings or emotions most of the time unconsciously. In this process, it is very likely that most of our fears are not our own but captured by our powerful antenna and taken as a reflection of our problems. Receiving an emotion of fear, the most common, resonates with conflicts, doubts and conditioning of our daily life. As a result these conditionings are adopted as our own when in reality they correspond to other persons or entities.

In places of agglomerations like stadiums, shopping malls or on the street you capture these negative energies of apprehension or uneasiness and associate them with your problems. If you have not learned how to detach yourself from these thoughts you will most likely get into patterns that lead you to create panic scenarios.

Fear and panic grow as we associate everyday events with the mind. If we are slaves of our mind in creating situations of suffering and pain, fear will always be present as a paralyzing sign of our own activity.

When our thinking wanders from past to future, we fall into the masochistic web of shocks and sorrows of an anarchic mind.

If you can always live in the present-now- here, you will enjoy an existence devoid of fears, terrors and panic, products of your creative capacity that acts in detriment of your physical and mental health. Much of the catastrophic circumstances that are yet to come are product of your logical mind as you play the future. They are storms that will never happen, beyond your pernicious imagination.

The expression of fear.

Many people express their fear through anger, rage, hatred, aggression, sadness and ultimately, depression. Otherwise not expressing his emotions the individual falls into isolation and depression, as well as physical and psychological disorders. By avoiding communicating his fear the person can become trapped and paralyzed with fear by these emotions. Sports, physical activity and yoga are disciplines that help eliminate the adrenaline generated by those negative feelings.

Inhibiting the expression of fear, like any other emotion, causes more damage than expressing it, because it ends up exploding in our organs or systems by producing diseases that are difficult to diagnose. The fear of living or existential anguish is the cause of multiple illnesses either because it manifests itself frequently or otherwise is somatized by preventing communication and overlaps that hide in the consciousness of the individual.

Fear and external agents.

Sometimes we fight against energy of fear that stubbornly repeats itself during the 24 hours of the day. We exclude that pernicious influence but it remains there in our psyche. The conclusion may focus on some entity that has penetrated the person's electromagnetic field and resides there.

Entities enter the field of the person for different reasons. When the person uses drugs or drinks liquor frequently.

The victim, in order to enter other dimensions, ingests hallucinogen products such as peyote, ayahuasca or yagé and Sanpedro. When the invaded person has been subjected to psychic attacks and/ or witchcraft or the individual possesses psychic faculties as a channel, it captures wandering spirits but often does not know it.

In these cases it is not enough to expel energy. It is required to eject the entity from the electromagnetic field of the person or place where there are physical vestiges of the body or elements used by the entity when it inhabited the earth.

These phenomena often occur in houses where someone was killed or tortured before dying or suffered physical and moral pain from a terminal illness. For the moment science does not endorse the existence of the spirit that is present in most mental illnesses. But according to Albert Einstein, energy is not extinguished, nor is it dissipated, but transformed. If we are energy, where does ours go when the body dies? Where does the vital energy that gives existence to a body reside?

For different reasons some spirits wander in the ocean of subsistence in dimensions close to ours where their attachment to earthly life does not allow them to continue their evolution in other frequencies and vibrations. Then they want to continue to enjoy life in terms of vice, bacchanals and sometimes inciting to kill or act as agents of evil in all its manifestations.

Not all spirits that hover around a person's electromagnetic field are bad. Sometimes the spirit of a relative enters the field to protect a child or simply when the family member suffers an attachment for the being that leaves the body.

Sometimes the spirit of a great character enters the body of a channel. This one manifests it in the form of a trance and acts as the spirit was in life, healing terminal illnesses or producing quantum physics phenomena called miracles.

For science these phenomena do not exist, but in the popular imagery of all cultures there is a war hidden by people who want to dominate others with tools invisible to the analytical eye of the researcher.

Fear and pain.

This is an emotion inherent to the human being since the time when it had to subsist in front of other animals and his own species. In the millions of years of human evolution, fear has always been considered a reaction to real or fictitious danger. It can be considered as a defense mechanism that unfolds in the consciousness in the face of a threat to survival.

Fear can be inserted in the past as a neurotic obsession with something that happened which deeply marked the psyche of an individual and that unconsciously triggers itself by mental association with matters that relate to painful events.

Fear is then necessary to some extent to preserve life because it prepares the individual to defend himself in moments of threat.

Psychological fear can be generated by the mind in situations that do not correspond to real danger. But the mechanism of thinking and imagining by superfluities and misconceptions can produce fear, or in the mental creation of unpleasant situations that the individual could live, a series of symptoms are triggered that both the body and the psyche of him undergo alterations that lead to pain. They are the imaginations that our mind creates from terror of facts that have not happened. It is anguish of living or surviving in this world of consumption and competition. Thus, the line between fear and pain becomes very tenuous, so much as to prey on an individual's fears and thus delivering a great deal of pain. In other words, fear leads to panic and this to pain.

Fear and separation from divinity.

When the human being does not believe in anything, in some form of energy or relies on any creed, it falls as easy prey of depression and modern illness.

We will not defend the religions that have helped some humans find their way because present life guides us towards a spiritual path beyond religions. They played a limited role in the mental, psychic and spiritual development of the planet but their mentors committed all sorts of excesses, managing to distort the purpose for which they were created: to give happiness to man.

However, being an agnostic or atheist does not contribute to the healing of the suffering and grief that humanity goes through. In philosophical discussions it is hard to prove the existence of God as Kant concluded. Nor will we resort to Feuerbach's theories in the sense that it was man who created God.

On the other hand, the word God has been used in many ways, so much that it has been reified and worn. Its meaning is far from the magnificence, infinity, goodness and power that encompassed everything. The truth is that in the name of God all kinds of injustices, abuses and crimes were committed in the ancient and recent history of mankind.

When you penetrate the mysteries of meditation in its different modalities or in deep prayer, you arrive after a process to the perception of energy inherent to each. A different energy that clothes you with the mantle of peace, tranquility and joy overflowing, or happiness per se. That unique and individual experience allows us to know by personal experimentation that in the depths of our psyche we are a sea of energy that some call divinity. In fact, they talk about saints who achieved through good religious practices, prayer or meditation, states of rapture and extraordinary pleasure at the level of the spirit. This state is attributed to being in the consciousness of the divinity.

The vast majority of fears we feel occur while being away from that divinity. Or put another way, when we contact our sea of inner energy we exorcise any kind of fear.

The modern society that has given so much importance to technological development and the creation of machines and robots that replace human work has made us victims of the ego. As the ego grows by the material achievements of man, it moves further away from its own sea of energy or divinity.

By moving away from its own identity, the human suffers by the absurd competition of modern life and by the parameters of happiness sold by television and the Internet. These parameters demand a constant struggle for survival that only ends with the death of the individual. Marshall McLuhan, Canadian philosopher, theorist and professor, already spoke in the sixties of "existential anguish" or desperation of living.

The separation of man from his own sea of energy, which is also experienced in the worship of divine teachers like Jesus, Buddha or Krishna, leaves the human of today at the expense of fears,

One of the most effective ways to erase fears that even seem to be so exacerbated is to seek the inner divinity that resides in each human being, to bathe in its supreme energy that will give him the power to guide all aspects of his life. Others find that energy in deep and faithful prayer.

When we perceive or experience pure inner energy, we free ourselves from all kinds of fears. This also implies the disappearance of the ego that identifies us with our possessions, talents, fame and additional arrogance.

Only in situations of despair when there is no solution to problems, man resort to his own inner energy through meditation or prayer, to find peace and mitigate his pain. It is the inner divinity that is responsible for eliminating all monsters that lurk inside, intuitively recognizing that the energy of the universes resides in you.

Fear and attachments.

Attachment is the dependence that human beings have in relation to people, material possessions, sex, and when consumption is moderate, to drugs or alcohol. Any stimulant that produces pleasure is likely to become an attachment.

Attachment carries fear and anxiety of losing the cause of that pleasure which leads to dependence.

The possibility that the object subject to attachment may vanish produces pain. The human must learn to let go of people or possessions so as not to get sick or upset when they leave his existence, because in this mutant and changing world everything can be extinguished. Then everything that gives us pleasure can be enjoyed with the security of eliminating the pain when it no longer exists.

In the same way you can love someone special without dependency that turns a positive feeling into hate and resentment. Many fears that remain latent belong to this category. For example, there are couples who endure all kinds of harassment for fear of losing the company of their beloved one or for fear of having to divide their material goods.

To possess is a distinctive trade of the ego and a disguise that conceals the true identity of being. The ego places the individual in the orbit of pleasure-pain: I enjoy it or suffer its absence and non-existence. This is the classic dilemma between being and having. But if we eliminate attachments it can be-and-have at the same time. It is not harmful to have material success; the issue is to enjoy it without attachments. But the priority is being.

Fear of loneliness is a product of attachment to the family, loved ones, the partner or the possibility of losing them. It is also a consequence of the separation of our being, our own divinity. Fear of leaving the comfort zone that appears permanently in our life is the typical attachment to circumstances, people and things that give us apparent stability but shut out the possibility for change and development. One way to always be optimistic and cheerful is to accept all variations that life proposes and allow the flow of events as an unopposed witness.

Power over others is also a source of attachment. When people come out of public life or lose positions of leadership, they suffer from depressions. The same happens when their fame and protagonism in the media is diluted.

There is a psychotic attachment to celebrities. Some fans love an artist or idol without knowing them and can act in a violent way if they do not yield to their pretensions of rapprochement or interrelation.

Rejection is an attachment that urges you to avoid a person, situation or environment that causes pain. The fear of pain, latent or active, stimulates this negative emotion. Rejection may be unconscious of its origin in early childhood or other lives. When the individual feels the danger of the situation then fear of the people or environments are triggered wherever the individual is. This emotion is sometimes hidden in the form of hatred or aversion. Under certain circumstances, fear is transformed into hatred and this into aggressive actions against the people or environments that triggered it. Only a detonator is required for this to explode.

THE PHOBIAS

When fear becomes obsessive and uncontrollable it is called a phobia. Most of the time fear is triggered by just thinking about the object that produces it. The situation that induces danger may well exist only in the imagination of the person who perceives it, which means that painful symptoms appear.

Psychoanalysts place the origin of phobias in the patient's relationships with their biological or foster parents. The persistence of phobia can lead to panic and extreme anxiety in the person.

Fear can appear by thought, in mental associations with the object or circumstances that trigger the phobia. The intimate substance of fear is physical death, annihilation, isolation or social death. Being in the here-now to find the reality of the infinite being that inhabits our cells is a useful tool to eliminate phobias and exorcise fears.

Present time is a formidable asset, a treasure we possess per se. Upon entering it, we receive all inner peace and energy that connects us with the universe. Being in the present frees us in those moments of fear that surround our conscience.

As noted earlier, fears are inherent to personality and reproduced in many ways. It is very difficult not to be exposed to their influence. They multiply by the media, the psychic environment of places, friends, family environment, work or study. They are also received through our electromagnetic field by transmission of any person who experiences them in a conscious or unconscious way. They are low frequency signals that penetrate our field because they are there close to our influence. A wave of thought encompasses more than 14,000 kilometers of instantaneous range.

When fears fade away by eliminating the resistance to experiencing them, they become positive action, vitality, energy, peace, and universal love; the most effective antidote.

We could infer that fears will always be there, but the secret is not to let them influence us or be paralyzed by them. By experiencing the peace and love that dilutes them, we can obtain from them a great amount of energy to act in the attainment of formidable results.

Anxiety, which is a fear involved with the results of a future event in a person's life, may be the catalyst for a greater fear beyond the category of panic. That is, if anxiety is not controlled the individual may end up paralyzed with terror and with severe symptoms at the body level. Anxiety creates more fear.

Worry is a less intense fear that can drain all your energy, by occupying your mind in the struggle with windmills that in reality do not exist. A brief concern serves to provide solutions to problems. When it is obsessive, it results in an enormous effort, an excessive and inane expenditure of energy that leads to neurosis. As an Eastern proverb says, "If a problem has no solution, why bother, but if it has a solution, why bother?"

INSTRUCTIONS ON HOW TO RELEASE FEARS

I change the registry: 'I'm afraid of' .... for:

I focus on solutions to counteract this fear

I commit to perform such actions to eliminate the fear of .....

I eliminate my perception of fear.....

I put my strongest intention in eliminating the fear of......

I have enough and permanent strength to eliminate the fear of....

I take from the Divine Source of All that is the force and intention to eliminate this fear of......

I bring to my life all things that help me overcome this fear or phobia. These actions allow me to live in harmony without fear:

I remove the resistance to eliminate this fear. Eloo!

I change this fear for self-confidence. Mona 'oha.

Fear is a lack of universal love.

I eliminate from my cells guilt and sin and with them the fear of being punished.

I remove regrets and remorse created by mistakes in my life.

I avoid persisting in the same error and command correction to my cells through love.

From my inner being I fill my psyche with confidence, to protect me in all events of my life, with love.

I identify myself without fear or phobia with....

I focus all my attention on feeling free of fears.

I remove the cause of fears that reside in wrongdoing, from the ego.

I let my feelings and emotions flow to manifest my inner happiness and peace.

I delete attachments to people or things and with it the fear of losing them.

My strong and firm intention is to live without fear when sending love to all beings.

I create my own reality free of any kind of fear. I train my mind to eliminate damaging others.

I have blind faith in my success in eliminating my fears by acting the right way.

I am determined to eliminate this fear of.........

I have confidence in God, The Creator of all that Is and in my angels that protect me in every situation.

I trust in the Divine Source of all that Is that resides within me and in the heart of humanity.

I have the strength and energy of God within me.

I have the strength, energy and intention of Jesus Christ to eliminate my fears and live fulfilled and happy.

I accept all the events in my life and make them the immanent happiness of Being.

I always act on the basis of the infinite being within me and avoid making decisions that are based on impure thoughts, negative feelings and low frequency emotions.

To love all beings, automatically erases my fears.

The confidence of my heart is born of my harmony with the universe.

I eliminate forever criticizing myself.

I avoid making the wrong decisions that make me feel guilty and afraid.

Here and now I am confident, strong and firm in love and peace.

I have faith in my intention, my strength, my confidence, my security and the love that emerges from my being to exorcize all my fears.

I eliminate the fear of .... in all my actions.

With confidence, strength, intention and love, I am my own teacher who overcomes all fears.

I am a great teacher lacking in nonessential fears.

I eliminate all mental structures and models that involve me with fear and hatred.

I pray and connect with the Divinity to exorcise my fears.

With this meditation, I remove my fears forever.

Being in the present - now helps me eliminate my fears.

I choose forever a life free from non-essential fears.

I remove all low frequencies and vibrations of fear from my being. I vibrate in constant love for everything and everyone.

By eliminating my fears I take a quantum leap in my evolution.

The feeling within me, the infinite being, eliminates my fears.

I isolate myself from the collective unconscious of low frequencies and vibrations of hatred and fear.

By sending universal love to all humans, I exorcise my fears.

If I have been wrong in my actions, I correct my conduct forever, I am a loving being.

I release the electric blockage in my physical body.

I eliminate all the blockages in my electromagnetic-gravitational field caused by fears.

I completely heal my psyche, body and spirit of fears.

I reject all the worries packaged in messages, readings, lectures, sermons, speeches, classes, stories or memes and fill them with love.

By eliminating fears I purify myself in perfection and love.

I clean my environment of negative emotions, thoughts or vibrations and transform them into peace, happiness and universal love.

With the power of my verb, strength, confidence and firm intention, I decree forever to exorcise the fear of....

I feel the divine grace within me.

We are all one through love, the fifth element. I feel free, I feel happy, I feel confident. I am capable of the greatest achievements.

With the divine energy that springs from my heart, I have eliminated all the fears that impeded my realization as a human being.

In deciding to never love, I caused fear to....

I eliminate all the mental forms and entities of fear that could be in my electromagnetic field. I always act in love for others.

Fear is born of my ego, in suppressing it, I am happy.

I change all my mental programs for wrong actions to feel the freedom in my being and erase my fears.

I erase all programs and beliefs associated with nonessential fear.

I live in the here-now with my infinite being.

With each breath I am in the now free of thoughts, emotions or feelings of the past or future.

I refuse to resist the events that occur in my life.

I vibrate in acceptance and tolerance for everything that happens in my life.

I am stronger by recognizing my weaknesses and fragility.

I dwell in the divine energy to enjoy the freedom of my inner being.

I am the power and glory of the divine source.

The above changes are recorded in the water element of my body for its transformation and health.

HOW TO DELETE REJECTIONS, HATES, RANCORS, RAGE.

I change the registry 'I hate, reject so and so', for:

I eliminate feeling offended by so-and-so.

I will not blame so-and-so.

I refuse to reject so-and-so.

I have taken away my resistance to accepting the facts.

I suppress judging so-and-so.

I delete criticizing so-and-so.

I remove punishing so-and-so.

I suppress condemning so-and-so.

I eliminate sentencing so-and-so.

I remove forever being offended by so-and-so.

I erase my resistance to forgiving so-and-so.

I have taken away my resistance to accepting the facts.

From the depths of my heart, from the depths of my soul, from the depths of my being and for my own good, I forgive and accept so-and-so as it is.

I delete the notion of hate from my cells.

I eliminate hating hatred. That is, to respond with hatred to anyone who hates or dislikes me.

I erase hate from my cycles of births and deaths.

I eliminate attachment to negative feelings such as hatred.

I eliminate the need to be right.

I eliminate the need to win.

I eliminate the need to feel superior.

From the depths of my heart, from the depths of my soul, from the depths of my being and for my own good, I forgive and accept so-and-so as it is.

From the bottom of my heart, from the depths of my soul, from the most intimate of my being, I send universal love for so-and-so.

I accept that I have learned lessons with so-and-so.

I accept the lessons that so-and-so gave me.

I accept the lessons my life gives me.

The divinity and I are one.

So and so and me are one.

If I attack with thought and hurt so-and-so, I hurt myself.

I remove war from my cells.

By sending universal love to so-and-so, I eliminate conflict, fear and hatred.

I remove feelings of revenge.

I eliminate the need to do justice by my own hand.

I swear by the law of karma where each action generates a reaction and I watch for my actions to always be good.

I eliminate all the structures and mental models that invite me to hate.

I raise the frequency and vibration of my being to emigrate from collective hatred.

I live my life in balance and universal love for all beings.

I have patience with so and so.

So-and-so's actions were dictated from his ego. I see in so-and-so, the infinite being, full of love.

I allow my feelings to flow.

I forever bless so-and-so for the lessons of life he gave me.

I have expelled from my electromagnetic field any hateful entity that has adhered.

By understanding the lessons of life that so-and-so gave me, I forever eliminate hatred, rejection, rancor, or anger toward him.

I eliminate hatred in every dimension that reaches my soul.

As I healed this negative feeling, I paved the way for my awakening and my own enlightenment.

I receive all the energetic models that heal my soul from hatred, rejection, resentment and anger.

My life is now filled with love and compassion.

My relationship with nature, animals, beings of other dimensions and the whole human race is full of love, solidarity and peace.

I eliminate hatred from my previous lives.

I eliminate the hatred of my ancestors.

I eliminate the hatred of my parents.

I migrate from the morphed field of hatred and disease.

I change the frequency of hatred of my cells for universal love of all that is.

I feel peaceful.

I feel calm.

I feel at ease.

I am in peace with everything and with everyone.

I accept that the experiences lived with so-and-so contribute to the purification and perfection of my being.

I am in peace with the universe.

I am in peace with so-and-so.

I thank God for this release.

I thank Jesus the Christ (Buddha, Krishna, Yahweh, Allah) for this deliverance.

I feel infinite compassion for so-and-so.

I feel unconditional love for so-and-so.

So-and-so is a being of light like me.

I communicate with so-and-so from my divine being to his divine being.

I thank the beings of light for this Healing.

I thank God the creator of all that is for this liberation and cleansing of my cells.

I feel free, I feel pure.

I purify my bodies, purify my spirit, and purify all aspects of my merkaba or body of light.

All these changes I register in the memory of the cells of my bodies forever.

An 'Anasha. Thank you.

I am the power and the glory from my being.

I register all these changes in the water element of my body for its transformation and health.

HOW TO ELIMINATE COMMOTION, ANXIETY AND PANIC.

I change the registry "I feel panic" for what is happening or has just occurred, for:

I clean these painful and negative emotions of my life and fill them with universal love from the center of my heart.

I change the commotion and panic for spiritual pleasure generated from my divine being.

Panic and anxiety is the product of the dual mind.

When eliminating negative thoughts, emotions and feelings, my infinite being reigns.

My being is present in the difficult moments of duality to put it aside and enjoy the beauty and love from within.

I breathe deeply to eliminate the obsession and panic of the situation.

Pleasure and pain change, the only immutable thing is the intimate and refulgent presence of the being.

I change panic and depression for joy, happiness and universal love from the bottom of my being.

I transmute sadness and pain in the overflowing joy of the inner being.

I feel the purity of my divinity that gives me security, confidence and strength.

I change fear, panic and anxiety for infinite peace and calm from my being.

I change abandonment by shelter, solidarity, affection and plenty of love lavished from my infinite being.

I remove forever the commotion and panic so that the splendor of my being shines forever.

I remove shock and anxiety so that the purity, strength and the eternal confidence of the being appear.

I eliminate fear and anxiety for the results of this situation.

I remove emotional shock and pain and fill them with the ocean of universal love.

In my psyche there is only ineffable happiness, the eternal bliss of being.

I am always guarded by my angels, the beings of light, Jesus the Christ, the avatars and my omnipotent being.

I accept that I learn lessons through commotion, panic and anxiety.

I breathe deeply to be in the presence of the infinite being.

I take away all forms of pain from my life.

I suppress the fear of pain and change it for the awareness of my pure and divine being.

I accept all the events in my life and transform them into the immanent happiness of being.

My present lessons are free from pain. I only receive light, love, happiness, divinity and the magical energy of being.

I suppress the fear of loneliness and impotence and change them through the penetrating love of being, security and trust.

I erase forever commotion, panic, anxiety and change them for the divine presence of the being.

I decree to always erase my turmoil, panic and anxiety from the situation I lived.

I fill every cell in my body with the splendor and exultant presence of being.

I ask my infinite being and the Divine Source of all that is to erase from my cells the impressions of shock and pain.

I vibrate in the frequency of zero concussion or anxiety.

I suppress the resistance to erase from my cells the commotion and panic of this situation.

I change identifying myself with anxiety for peace, joy and authentic happiness of being.

I eliminate attaching to negative emotions like panic, anxiety and commotion.

I concentrate my attention on eliminating commotion, panic, anxiety and changing them for peace and serenity of the present that emerges from the center of my heart.

I eliminate grudges, anger and hatred caused by my anxiety and commotion.

My emotions, thoughts and feelings flow like a river that leads to the finite sea of universal love that is in the present-now.

I eliminate the guilt's that could cause me commotion and anxiety and the change them for abundance, spiritual wealth and full realization of the being.

I have the firm intention to erase commotion, panic and anxiety.

Accepting the lessons learned is part of my spiritual growth and evolution.

My goal is to leave the pleasure-pain duality to always live in the magical energy of being.

The elimination of commotion and anxiety gives me the tranquility to face the course of life.

I transmute panic and shock for peace and happiness from the infinite being.

I regret feeling victimized by panic, commotion and anxiety experienced. I am free and as such I fully enjoy existence.

I free myself from all the prejudices caused by panic and commotion. I love all beings without exception.

I am my own master who overcomes all his panics. I am an infinite being full of kindness and benevolence.

I ask the divine source of all that is, to free myself from the aftermath of anxiety and pain.

I choose forever that the cells of my bodies are free of pain.

I live and always breathe universal and infinite love.

I apologize and accept all the people involved in commotion, panic and anxiety.

I only have thoughts of gratitude, peace and inner love for all beings.

I purify all my bodies of negative and low-frequency energies.

I build an environment of harmony, solidarity and compassion for others.

Through breathing I am always living in the now.

I enjoy the wonderful energy that emanates from being within me.

I appreciate everything that comes into my life.

I thank the Divine Source of all that is, the releasing of panic, commotion and anxiety from the cells of my bodies.

With absolute faith in my powers, I am totally free from these negative emotions.

I feel divine grace in me. I enjoy the exultant energy of infinite being.

I expel from my electromagnetic field all the low-frequency energies I receive from the outside and send them to the divine field of thought for its transformation and evolution.

By the grace and love of Jesus Christ I remove commotion, panic and anxiety from all my body cells.

I register all these changes in the water element of my physical body for its health and evolution.

DEPRESSION

I eliminate the lack of my psyche when I contact with my infinite being that contains everything.

I erase the sadness for the lack of someone in my life. I am content and accompanied when I am aware of my infinite being.

When I feel the completeness of my being, I can make happy those who accompany me, by giving them the purity of my love.

I eliminate the lack of interest in everything, when I realize that inside me the pure essence of life itself pulsates.

I eliminate love with pain or attachment to people, things, animals, power, wealth or fame.

I cast out my ego to live in the harmony of my infinite, divine and pure being.

By suppressing the ego I feel the power and infinite wisdom of Being.

I possess everything I need to be very happy, when I contact the divinity that resides in the infinite being.

I have everything I desire in the eternal present-now in the expansion of my infinite being as pure divinity.

In this holographic world, within my being I possess in each and every one of my cells, a fractal of pure energy of the divine source of all that is.

I am a holographic sample of God the Creator.

I am always connected to the divine source of love and compassion.

The outside world is a fiction; the reality that creates everything is the infinite Being.

The pleasures offered by the ego are fleeting; the inscrutable bliss of being is immutable and eternal.

Nothing is more beautiful than the creations of being.

By suppressing the ego's cravings, I eliminate depression and sadness.

I erase forever the guilt from my cells. Guilt exists only in the ego.

I erase all hatreds so that my pure love for others always shines. Hate is a feeling of the ego.

When the ego disappears I receive the great energy of the being which gives me happiness, strength and power to live in harmony at all times.

As I feel my infinite being, my fatigue disappears and I completely heal my soul.

I always breathe concentrating my attention on the heart –Chakra, in the beautiful energy that expands like a sun.

I feel the happiness of being in each and every one of the trillions of cells of my bodies.

Sadness and depression only exist in the ego. I eliminate these feelings and negative emotions to sense the purity of Being.

I focus on my master of light, pray to God and feel the answer in my Heart-Chakra as a sensation of happiness and fulfillment.

I meditate on Elexier, the divine love, and I feel it in every cell of my bodies.

I imagine being in the most beautiful environment of this world. (A forest, a garden, a beach). I feel how I connect with the infinite being through nature and the inherent happiness of being. Pause to imagine.

Being with nature captures the Prana or subtle energy that lives in all beings. I fill my body with that energy to be full and happy.

Being in pure and universal love I declare my ego non-existent.

I recover the natural joy that comes from being. In this reality I am the ineffable happiness.

Being in pure and universal love I dissipate all griefs, sorrows and depressions.

To always live in the high vibration of the infinite being I first heal my mind of thoughts, emotions and feelings of low frequency.

I disappear all creations of the ego such as sufferings and pain to live always in the glory of the infinite being.

When I heal my mind, the ego disappears.

The Infinite being is the highest expression of pure love within me.

I remove all judgments and reasons that give life to this depression.

I erase my beliefs that there is only the three-dimensional world and my body, to feel that there are other dimensions in the psychic world and that pure love lives in my heart.

I am something more subtle and transcendent than this body in which I dwell.

The Divine thought replaces the ego. I focus my attention on pure thoughts, feelings, and emotions.

I feel the divine grace within me. I live the peace and harmony of the infinite being.

By suppressing the ego I leave the chaos that reigns in my mind to enter into the bliss and calm of the omnipresent being.

The depression that makes me suffer helps me to find the answer through the elimination of the ego and the awakening to the liberation of duality, to live in the supreme bliss of infinite being.

HOW TO RELEASE GUILT

I remove forever the original sin from my cells.

I erase from my cells the notion of sin, guilt, and error.

Error is a source of growth and evolution.

Errors are lessons learned.

I delete to persist in the same error.

I eliminate punishment for making mistakes.

I remove punishment for guilt and sin.

Life is governed by the law of cause and effect. I reap everything I sow.

If I sow hate and resentment I reap pain and suffering. If I sow love I reap love and happiness in abundance.

I eliminate sin and guilt from my cells.

I eliminate the guilt attributed to me by others.

I forgive myself.

I receive forgiveness from the divine source of all that is.

I cleanse my cells of sins, iniquities and mistakes and fill them with love.

I fill my cells with prosonodo light, the most powerful light of all planes of existence, transmitted by Jesus Christ.

I eradicate remorse from my conscience.

I erase regrets from my conscience.

I eliminate diseases caused by my faults.

I eliminate failures caused by my faults.

I cast the guilty entity out of my electromagnetic field.

I reject guilt's, fears of punishment, and the sins and errors transmitted by any means of communication.

I reject the memes of guilt transmitted by pastors, priests and politicians.

I eliminate the sermons or speeches that accuse me as guilty.

I am free from guilt, sins and mistakes.

I accept the mistake and take their lessons without feeling guilty.

I eliminate the sins, guilt's and errors of my ancestors.

I erase the sins, guilt's, and errors of my previous lives forever.

I remove from the genetic level the mistakes, sins and faults of my parents.

I suppose sin, guilt and error as a psychological form of punishment.

I emigrate forever from the morphed field of guilt.

I suppress the fear of punishment that causes disease.

I overturn the fear of punishment that causes failure.

I forgive myself and accept myself as I am.

I love myself and accept myself as I am.

I am free from the chains of guilt.

I avoid vibrating in the frequency of guilt.

I receive every energetic model that heals my soul of guilt's, errors and sins.

I feel clean.

I feel pure.

I love myself.

I feel worthy of all the good and wonderful of this life.

I eliminate all mental structures and models pointing towards me as guilty.

I am freed from sins, guilt's and errors.

I suppress blaming myself.

I eliminate blaming others for the facts of my life.

I remove criticizing myself.

I eliminate punishing myself.

I suppress judging myself.

I eliminate guilt in all dimensions my soul reaches and in all strata of my soul.

I feel clean and crystalline like pure water.

I feel worthy of all the good and wonderful of this life.

I deserve to live the happiness of the present-now.

I deserve to feed my cells with the Prana of air, earth, water, fire, Light and sound.

I deserve to feed myself with the Prana of universal love.

I deserve to enjoy the pleasure of sex.

I create wonderful things for my life.

I deserve to give and receive much love.

I deserve to give and receive tenderness.

I deserve to give and receive sweetness.

I deserve the love and power of energy.

I deserve the love of God, the creator of all that is.

I deserve the happiness that sex generates.

I receive all the love of divine energy.

I receive all the love of God and of the people.

I give all the love to God and the people.

I deserve all the good and wonderful of this life.

I deserve the health of my bodies, my soul, my spirit.

I deserve abundance and wealth.

I am one with God the Creator of all that is.

I eliminate punishment from my life.

I eliminate pain from my life.

I create a healthy life without pain.

I deserve a healthy life free from pain.

I am free from all forms of pain.

I emigrate forever from the morphed field of guilt. I live in freedom and the absolute happiness of being.

I avoid toxic people who foist faults on others.

I accept all the events of my life, without struggle and resistance, from my absolute present in communion with my Being.

I am innocent, pure and clean.

I have the power of love and divine energy.

I eliminate forever the resistance to erase guilt. Eloo!

By eliminating forever sins, guilt's and errors from my cells, I start my awakening.

I remove all locks from the electrical circuits in my physical body.

I remove all the blockages in my electromagnetic field caused by pain, guilt, hatred and fear in this and other lives.

I unblock my electromagnetic and gravitational field to travel free through the dimensions of the infinite Being.

I am the power and the glory of the divine source.

I am on the right path to my enlightenment.

I register all these changes in the water element of my body for its transformation and health.

* Prosonodo light can only be transmitted by a Sol'A'Vana of Kryon Master.

HOW TO RELEASE ATTACHMENTS

I change the registry 'I feel attached to' ....for:

I eliminate attachments from my cells. I remove love with pain from my cells.

I suspend my mind to be in the now, in the presence of being.

I erase identification with my ego.

I experience unity with all that is. El'noras.

I eliminate my attachment (sick love) to people.

I suppress my attachment, love with pain, to my loved ones.

I co-create love without pain in my relationships.

I co-create love without suffering in my interpersonal relationships.

I co-create love without griefs.

I co-create love without regrets.

I co-create love without remorse.

I co-create love free of guilt.

I co-create love without obsession.

I co-create love with ample space and freedom.

I am free of commitments, promises, contracts, oaths and vows in this and other lives to feel freedom and universal love. Lay'o'esha.

I am tolerant of other people's mistakes and I eliminate hate or rejection in response.

By loving others I accept all their qualities and limitations.

Nothing compels me to live with someone full of vices or irreversible defects.

I eliminate toxic people from my life.

I help others to change their defects by virtue.

I have clarity that the Divinity lives in me, when I put out my mind and my ego.

I am inexorably united to the Divinity.

I co-create unselfish love in other people.

I eliminate manipulating others to obtain their love.

I eliminate possession of my loved ones.

My loved ones are beings of light.

I eliminate dominion over my loved ones.

True love is full of trust, spaciousness and freedom.

I eliminate identifying with my possessions and goods.

I eliminate identifying myself with fame.

I eliminate identifying with my achievements and feats.

I remove possession and selfish love for my belongings.

I eliminate love with pain or attachment to my belongings.

I remove possession of my pets. I delete attachment to my pets.

I eliminate attachment to my work.

Life is governed by change. I accept changes in my life. I adapt to those changes.

I remove attachment to my mother.

The soul does not die, it only changes habitat. I communicate with my loved ones in any dimension where they are.

I express love to my loved ones in the dimension where they are.

I remove attachment, love with pain, to my father.

I suppress attachment to my siblings.

I eliminate attachment to sites, houses, environments.

I delete attachment to my toys.

I give the best of me to my loved ones.

I give the best of me to my 'enemies'. I send compassion to whoever hurts me.

I eliminate all mental structures and models that lead me to attachment.

I eliminate mistrust and jealousy in my emotional relationships.

When love is pure, relationships flow.

If a love relationship is about learning and pain, it is healthy to separate when there are no more lessons to learn from that person.

All my separations are full of love for the other.

I clean all memories of rejections, hatreds, resentments and envy, of my ex-partner.

I clean the relational field with my ex-partner so that peace, harmony and universal love reign.

I seek the happiness of my partner.

I suppress the pain when my partner is distant, for love from the most intimate of my being.

I remove pain when a loved one leaves this world. We are all connected. I will always communicate with my loved one at will.

I co-create love without aggression.

I remove myself from being a victim or a victimizer of my partner.

I give and ask respect from my partner.

I send thoughts of kindness and benevolence to all my loved ones in all dimensions and all circumstances.

I eliminate selfish feelings with all beings.

I meditate every day to be centered in my inner divinity.

I wish all the best to my loved ones when they leave my life.

I eliminate feeling the abandonment of God and the separation of the Divine source.

I eliminate resistance to suppressing attachments.

I suppress attachments that bind me to my mind, to evolve towards an awakened and enlightened being.

I turn off my mind, silence my ego. I focus my attention on eliminating my attachments.

I firmly intend to eliminate my attachments.

I have absolute faith in eliminating my attachments.

I choose to suppress my attachments.

By erasing my attachments, my Divine Being emerges.

By eliminating my attachments, I raise my vibration and my frequency.

By erasing my attachments I vibrate with God the Creator of all that is.

By eliminating my attachments I purify myself and advance with my soul into new dimensions of universal love.

I bless my Divine Being for suppressing my attachments for real and lasting happiness.

I decree with my verb that I have suppressed all my attachments.

I feel how divine grace floods my aspects of the body of light.

I am a merciful being.

I release all the locks in my electromagnetic and gravitational fields generated by attachments.

God is all. We are all God, Divine Energy.

I am the power and glory of the divine source.

All these changes are recorded in the water element of my body for its transformation and health.

EMOTIONAL PAIN, VIOLATION

Having the awareness of the infinite Being I remove the emotional pain caused by the violation of my body.

I eliminate any pain that may remain in my psyche by sending energy to all my cells from the infinite being.

I remove the pain and shock of that event that exists only in duality and the ego.

I erase feeling victimized by others in my ego-mind.

I erase the feelings of vengeance that exist in duality.

I eliminate the need to do justice by my own hand.

I know that with this experience of my pleasure-pain duality, I am balancing my karma in this life.

I eliminate the fears of being alone in an intimidating environment; I always walk with my infinite being and my teacher of light.

I eliminate anxiety and fear of having sexual intimacy.

I eliminate the guilt from my cells to enjoy the pleasure of sex.

I feel physical and spiritual pleasure in my sexual relationships.

From the depths of my heart, from the depths of my soul, from the depths of my being, I forgive and accept the aggressor who committed that abuse.

I accept that I have learned great lessons from that event in my life.

I accept the lessons life gives me.

I center my energy on my infinite being and observe the pain and pleasure of duality, as something transient.

I suspend my ego to be in the celebration of my infinite being.

From my infinite being that experience is a lesson in life.

I suppress judging the person (s) who perpetrated that act.

I refrain from criticizing the person who committed that act.

I erase all sexual prohibitions of my psyche to feel the freedom of my being.

I erase the emotional embarrassment that this fact caused me.

I refrain from blaming that person.

I eliminate punishing that person

I eliminate hatred, revenge and pain that bind me to that person.

I cleanse the relational field with So-and-so, to eliminate all negative feelings and fill it with the universal love that springs from my infinite being.

I erase the guilt of my cells and change them by universal love from the infinite being within me.

I remove the hatred that binds us in other lives to free me and free so-and-so forever, from my pure being of love.

I am free of karmas with so-and-so.

With the sword of Excalibur I decree absolute freedom of the spirit of so-and-so to find his way of universal love.

With the sword of Excalibur I cut off any karmic bond with so-and-so to enjoy my full freedom.

I eliminate the sinful connotation of sex, to feel it as an experience full of love and happiness.

I put an end to the aggressions and attachments with so-and-so.

I decree to have released forever the hatred that tied me in other lives and in this, with so and so.

I receive all the energy models that heal my soul from physical attacks and rape.

I feel calm, I feel at peace, I am at peace with so and so and I receive with love the past actions.

Peace in my soul. Peace in all the cells of my bodies.

I free myself from the emotional pain and trauma that these events produced in my cells.

I cleanse all the negative emotions of this experience and fill them with universal love.

I change the pain and trauma that remained in my duality and I transmute it to peace from my divine being.

Pleasure and pain are illusory; the only perennial thing is the infinite love that resides in my interior, in my true self.

I decree to eliminate forever the painful lessons of my life.

Everything that has happened in my life contributes to the purification and perfection of my being.

HOW TO DELETE EMOTIONAL PAIN

I change the registry 'I feel pain and trauma for the events that occurred in my past', for:

I clean all the negative and painful emotions of my life and fill them with universal love.

I change pain and emotional trauma for spiritual pleasure.

Pain is an illusion of the dual world as pleasure.

I feel the magical energy of my being.

I feel the overflowing joy of being.

My being has always been and is present in the difficult moments of my life.

Pleasure and pain change, the only invariable thing is the purity of my being.

I change weeping, sadness and depression for joy, happiness and plenty unconditional love.

I transmute depression into overflowing joy and supreme bliss of being.

I feel the purity of my divinity that gives me confidence and strength.

I change rage and aggression, for peace and calm from my being.

I change abandonment for shelter, affection and much love from my being.

I remove forever the pain and trauma, so that the divinity of my being shines in its entire splendor.

I remove trauma so that the purity, the strength and the eternal confidence of the being appear.

I eliminate pain and emotional shock and fill it with the ocean of universal love.

In my psyche there is only the ineffable happiness of being.

I have always been guarded by my angels, the beings of light, Jesus Christ and my omnipresent being.

I accept that I learned lessons through pain and trauma.

I eliminate forever from my life all forms of pain.

I suppress the fear of pain and change it for consciousness in my pure and divine being.

I accept all the events that occur in my life and make them the immanent happiness of being.

My present lessons are free from pain. I only receive light, universal love, divinity and the magical energy of being.

I erase the fear of loneliness and impotence and change it for security, trust, penetrating and eternal love of being.

I decree to always erase emotional pain and transmute it in the divine presence of being.

I erase the memory of pain and fill my body's cells with the presence of being.

I ask the universe to erase forever this pain or trauma from my cells and my bodies.

I vibrate in the zero emotional pains frequency and perfect healing of my subtle bodies.

I eliminate the resistance to erase forever the emotional pain, shock, and trauma that this situation gave me.

I change forever identifying myself with the pain and trauma of the situation I lived, for peace and the joy of being.

I project in others the image of a person free of trauma and emotional pain.

I eliminate my attachment to negative emotions such as pain and trauma.

I concentrate my attention on eliminating my emotional pains and traumas and changing them for the joy and happiness of living the present forever.

I remove grudges associated with my emotional pain.

My emotions, thoughts and feelings flow like a river that leads to the infinite sea of universal love that is in the absolute present.

I erase the guilt that emotional trauma or pain could generate and change it for abundance, spiritual richness and full realization of being.

My intention now is to eliminate emotional pain and accept the lessons learned as part of my process of growth and evolution.

My goal is to suppress the duality of pleasure and pain, to always live in the purity of being.

The elimination of emotional pain leads me to successful interpersonal relationships.

I transform the energy of pain and emotional shock to peace and spiritual pleasure from the infinite Being.

I discard feeling victimized by the pain I have experienced. I am a blessed person who enjoys life to the fullest.

I free myself from all the prejudices caused by emotional trauma. I love all beings.

I am my own master who overcame all his traumas. I am an infinite being full of compassion and benevolence.

I ask the Divine Source of all That Is, to free myself from all the aftermath of trauma and pain.

I choose forever that my cells remain free of pain and trauma. I live and always breathe in infinite love.

I forgive and accept all people involved in the incubation of emotional pain.

I only have positive thoughts of trust, security and inner peace.

I purify my body, mind, spirit, and emotional body from negative and low frequency energies. I build an environment of peace, harmony and universal love.

I always live in the eternal present. I enjoy the energy that emanates from the infinite being within me.

I appreciate everything that comes into my life. I am grateful for the release from emotional trauma and pain.

With absolute faith in my divine energy, I am completely healed of emotional pain.

I feel divine grace in me. I enjoy the exultant energy of being.

I cast out from my electromagnetic field all the negative energies I receive from the outside and send them to the divine field of thought for its evolution and transformation.

By the grace of Jesus Christ, I erase the trauma and pain from my cells.

We are all connected to the infinite Being; we are all the infinite being of love and compassion.

PART TWO

BIO PHOTONS

The human body emits bio photons, also known as ultra-weak photon emissions (UPE), with a visibility 1.000 times lower than the sensitivity of the naked eye. These bio photons help communication within the human environment. The bio photon is a quantum of light. They are released through mental intention and may modulate fundamental processes within cell-to-cell communication and DNA. According to GreenMedinfo, both the physical eye and the 'mental' eye emit ultra-weak photons that affect the cells of nature and the environment surrounding the human emitter. These rays can be measured with light-sensitive devices. These light emissions are correlated with cerebral energy metabolism and oxidative stress within the mammalian brain.

In the same publication, it is said that a recent study found that in a very dark environment where subjects actively imagined light, *their intention* produced significant increases in ultra-weak photon emissions out of the brain, although the production of bio photons is greater inside the brain than out of it during visual perception and imagination.. This explains the communication between living organisms. Light excites the nervous system with transmitted information.

Lynne McTaggart states in 'The Intention Experiment', that according to experiments taken to the laboratory by Rosebbaum and Sayantani Gosh, all particles communicate with each other in the subatomic world through non-local communication that allows them to connect regardless of distance or conditions of each particle. It is this testing in laboratory that proves we can all be connected by light emitted.

This teaches us that particles are entangled with each other through incessant communication. And this would explain how DNA is modified by orders given to human cells that receive or reproduce information transmitted at very low frequencies, undetectable by today's devices.

We influence everything around us: our partners, our children, the crowd in the mall, plants, and animals.

If a healer's thoughts are emitted as frequencies, *the intention* to heal is an orderly light with little interference, says McTaggart. *Intention* transforms the disordered mess of subatomic communication into an orderly and powerful transmission, like a laser.

Konstantin Korotkov, Russian scientist, inventor of Gas Discharge Visualization Technology, made several experiments in order to demonstrate that all living beings are susceptible to send and receive signals of light, which explains how plants, animals and microorganisms communicate.

If the *intention* is accompanied by love, compassion or empathy towards the recipient, it is more effective to transmit data from one mind to another or from a mind to a body.

In the intention to heal the attitude of the receiver is very important. If he/she has confidence and conviction in the effectiveness of the process, healing will be successful. Healing others helps heal the same emitter of light.

Empathy.

In the experiments performed to measure the effectiveness of healing it has been found that it is vital to establish an empathic communication between the healer and the subject receiving the healing. In remote transmissions one can obtain empathy by *ho'oponopono* exercises with a photo of the receiver. If there is no emotional or empathic bond between the two, healing is less effective unless there is the strongest intention on the part of the emitter-healer. In general terms, when someone empowers another to heal, a stream of thankfulness flows from the receiver to the healer. At other times, there may be a feeling of universal love for whom is going to perform healing, but the power of the healer's *intention* prevails over other factors. When prayer is offered, empathy is necessary; in other healing methods this is effective without the authorization of the recipient, according to experiments performed.

Quantum space.

In experiments carried out by William Tyler and narrated by McTaggart, it was shown that the human mind can accelerate the process of laboratory fruit flies growth through the human intention conveyed by meditators. But the interesting thing is that in the place where the experiments were realized, a quantum field was formed that accelerated the growth of the fly larvae even without the intervention of the meditators. A proof that the mind of the experimenter modifies to its will the result of the experiment and changes the conditions of the electromagnetic field where the experiments are made. In other words, the human mind modifies the space around it.

This would explain why in some places of worship such as churches, mosques and temples, the energy produces peace and calm, even when they are empty. In short, the human mind modifies the environment where the person is even to a greater extent if it has a trained mind or possesses psychic powers. And what is remarkable, the changes remain in space.

The imagination.

The intention is more effective in that it involves more senses in the moment of giving orders to the universe. A person who desires success in business for example, *will imagine beforehand* signing the contract, receiving the money in the bank, buying or doing things with that money, delving into new businesses or sharing with joy all these things with loved ones. If these moments are vivid in your imagination, the energies you move from the universe are more powerful. Imagine the situation with all detail: condition and particulars of the place where the business will take form, the favorable reaction of the people involved in the business and the celebration after the fruitful completion. All these thoughts will fill the space with orders to the universe to crystallize that reality. Imagination is a component that adds strength and power to intention. The emission of bio photons increases when the mind is filled with episodes that are experienced with the intensity of an action film and with total immersion of the senses. The knowledge of the location or place where the action will take place will also contribute to give more realism to the intention.

Recalling bitter facts causes havoc in the body because it follows the line of influence of the mind. Everything that happens in our mind has a chemical, neural and electromagnetic response in the body. In the same way, to evoke splendid moments of pleasure of the senses in pleasant experiences has a positive response by segregating dopamine, oxytocin, ephedrine and other hormones that produce joy in the body.

In the same book, McTaggart shows that when intention is full of positive thoughts, it works best in the presence of the subject to heal, but when the intention is negative, such as exterminating the microorganisms that form a tumor or kill cancer cells, it is more effective at a distance. Like curses, psychic attacks or witchcraft, it has an effect at a distance from its victims.

Break the barrier of time.

In quantum physics experiments, it has been proven that changing or manipulating a result in the future can modify the cause that originated said result. In fact, in healing we can modify a painful hatred towards the mother, going to the past and altering the conditions that produced that negative feeling from the present day that is the future of that event, to eliminate aggressive behaviors of the individual. We return to the past and justify the actions of the mother by the events that happened later in the individual's life, which in turn generated necessary adaptation learning lessons for life. There is a transgression of time because from the future we modify the past to change the present of an individual. The result is the elimination of the feelings and emotions on which the individual's neurotic and depressive nature was based. This practice requires a powerful intention on the part of the healer to act in the cleansing of past emotions that still remain in the psyche of the individual and the compliance of the same to obtain a positive response today.

The final effect is healing or erasing the negative feelings and emotions that overwhelmed him. We affect and transform the past because consciousness is independent of space and time.

The human mind through its thoughts, feelings, emotions and beliefs affects everything that is around it. We are equally touched by the thoughts and consciousness of other people, by the objects and things that keep memories of the emotions of individuals, plants and animals that live with us and the universe. We are inexorably linked to everything and with our conscious intention or not, we influence all things and other humans.

We possess an invisible force for the external senses and for that reason we doubt its existence. But this force is a power that acts independently of the conscious desires of a person. If someone is obsessed with fear of dying in an accident, they will focus all their intention on making those thoughts come true.

It is very likely that the accident will happen one day or another. The mind is a bomb that can be used for or against each of us, according to the positive or negative thoughts that it shelters. Hence the importance of erasing all the harmful emotions, feelings and beliefs that are harbored in it, understanding that they are the seed of involuntary thought-forms that can later harm us. Adequate suggestion and motivation of the mind propels us to do incredible feats by relying on the infinite power of our consciousness connected with a brilliant mind, trained in addition to discard pessimism, depression and all negative emotions. Always, and at any moment, we have the ability to decide which thoughts we emit: Either to continue with pessimistic or negative imagination musings that emerge as tragic or painful results or otherwise choose positive thoughts that create stories of triumph and happiness. We have the rudder and the control of channels. We tune into drama and pain or happiness, success and health.

The choice is always ours: before any fact of life, we decide to surrender to the tragedy or we take refuge in our inner infinite being that always emanates happiness, independent of what happens in the outside world.

By using the instructions in this book designed to heal the mind, it is obvious that we turn to the strongest intention to be effective in our goal. *Intention* is the axis on which we move in order to be assertive, efficient and effective in the process of clearing the consciousness of all the weeds and unwanted things that have arisen in the becoming of our own existence.

THE THOUGHT-FORMS

To dominate the mind through the different forms of meditation taught by the oriental cultures is apparently simple in practice, but to control the mind in our own activity is a dilemma not solved in its totality. Some Zen techniques teach us to meditate on the activity. But when our psyche is full of scars from the wounds received or produced, we easily enter into a psychic loop or wrapping obsession that dominates us and forces thoughts to be bound for a long time. These thoughts fill us with suffering and pain. We imagine scenes in the future plagued with horror, affliction and anguish. It is the existential anguish of which Herbert Marcuse spoke in the 60's that created this wild capitalism. The mind can be better controlled when we have cleansed it of those feelings, emotions or petty and harmful beliefs.

The thinking forms we produce are nourished by what the 5 senses transmit us and the filter that lives in layers in our unconscious. This is why it is easy to bring around hatred by watching a movie in which they rape someone or steal from people or trample and murder family members of the characters; because it resonates with the feelings and emotions that we have stored in our unconscious of this or other lives or transmitted by the genetics of our parents or our ancestors. So in order to control my mind I must first perform asepsis or cleaning up of all the psychological crap that I have in me.

Thought-forms are powerful antimatter that becomes reality by repeating them constantly. Fight or argue violently and hurtfully with someone and you will think about that person 24 hours a day. Why? Because it resonates with old feelings that you keep in the layers of negative thought- forms in your unconscious and the action becomes a psychological hook or permanent obsession. You feel hurt, offended and humiliated. It is what you keep inside even if the other person did not intend to hurt you that way. The thought-forms come true; this is why we always have to produce positive and optimistic thoughts of health, wealth and happiness in a psyche clean of impurities. So the power of thinking does not discriminate whether something is good or not. Think about something all the time and make it come true.

Do you understand many of the events in your life? And why should the psyche be cleaned? If I am obsessed with a good or bad event, at any moment it becomes a 3 dimensional truth, like extraordinary events of our life or physical accidents.

In this order of ideas, the first person to be healed is the mother. We have been in her womb and we have fed on all her emotions during the gestation stage. By healing the mother we heal 60 or 70 percent of our unconscious. The mother, said Sathya Sai Baba, is a free sample of the divine energy that resides within us. In having a pernicious or harmful relationship with the mother we are rejecting our own divine energy or we face and deny that same energy. In other words, we deny ourselves. The worst feeling that a human can hold is to hate oneself.

THE LAWS OF THE UNIVERSE TO REPEAT ONE EVERY DAY

1. I eliminate my resistance so that everything happens.

2. I focus my attention on my inner happiness.

3. I ask the universe for prosperity, benevolence and inner happiness.

4. I am always positive and optimistic.

5. I change all my defects by virtue.

6. I remove judging and criticizing others.

7. I detach myself from feelings, possessions or people.

8. I allow my feelings and possessions to flow.

9. I deserve abundance and draw it into my life.

10. I want to be successful in/with

11. My intention now is to be absolutely happy.

12. I think, speak and act as a prosperous and kindly being.

13. I want to be abundant, benevolent; to travel and to realize my Being.

14. I believe in myself, I have confidence in my actions and blind faith in myself.

15. I am very happy now.

16. I have learned the lessons. I do not come back to incarnate to learn.

17. I am responsible for myself and my actions.

18. I act according to my inner Self and my intuition.

19. I am a great teacher of life with inner happiness, peace and abundance to share.

20. I offer a prayer of love, peace and exuberance.

21. I listen and hear the voice of the universe.

22. I am a vibration of love, consciousness of being, joy of life and eternal present.

23. I am enlightened. I live in unconditional love. I materialize miracles.

24. I purify my body, my mind, my soul. My being purifies the environment and the people in it. I delete negative influences.

25. Everything is exuberance, love and happiness.

26. I am grateful for everything. I thank the universe for everything that flows in me.

27. I bless my life. I fully share Prosonodo divine light with everyone I know. I bless all places and beings with love and compassion.

28. I Decree exuberance, realization of the Self, compassion and happiness in all the acts of my life.

29. I have absolute faith in my enlightenment.

30. I am my own teacher full of grace, mercy, and wisdom.

31. I am my own healer.

32. We are all one. We come from the same divine source. God is love, he is one and we are all God.

ELIMINATE THE EGO OR SURRENDER

To surrender means blocking the negative influence of the ego, so that my true self, my essence, my substance, can come through. When we say 'I surrender', we refer exclusively to the ego. The ego is the false identity that speaks for me and has banal interests, worldly attachments and keeps me in the bipolarity of good-bad, smart-basic, black-white etc. the ego suffers from whims that, being dissatisfied, create pain. The ego revolves around the world of pleasure and earthly pain.

When we transcend the ego, there arises a sense of inner peace that cannot be compared to the pleasures of the senses. It is a perennial, immovable peace. It is an ending to all strife; the suppression of the world's battles to achieve goals. The body and mind are invaded by a total sense of surrender. A feeling of total selflessness, detachment and even unconcern from all the daily activities and surroundings.

Then the being floats in space and the will does not exist... This is the real flow with the river of life. It is as if an invisible hand were to surround my life. Like a feeling of protection from another dimension while eliminating all types of responsibility in the outcome of the action and accepting the result of it. It is the sensation of total freedom, without judgments, without analysis. Being in an absolute present free of pressures. It is to eliminate the importance of facts that are dwarfed by the magnitude and magnificence of the Being.

The Being is taken to the conscience and subtracts importance to the facts. There arises an avalanche of love that invades the whole consciousness which in turn stops acting in the rush to achieve results and goals. It is a total irrelevance of the vital facts by the magnificence of being.

It is surrendering to something higher that reigns in a greater phase of self-consciousness. It means that relevant things are not really so. It is allowing the flow of a higher energy that transcends all things; submitting to the magnificence of a master-God like Jesus Christ or any super-master. Or to surrender and bow before the all-governing Supreme Energy. It is to eliminate the clouds, storms and the worst tortures that threaten us, to give way to the Divine Source of all Creation. It is to enter into the total neutrality that emanates from the Source to dissolve the duality of the ego that qualifies facts and existence into two opposites: pleasure and pain, love and hate, good and bad.

In surrender and renunciation, any pain for the elimination of the ego ceases so that the pleasure of universal love shines in all its intensity; the eternal bliss of being, and the effulgent emanation of the I Am.

It is then that time stops to enjoy the eternal present as a fourth dimension and merges with being. Being and present are the same substance. Being, present, unity with everything; absolute connection with the transcendent universe. All and nothing in a single container; Emptiness and everything in the same body wrap.

Letting in, letting go.

In the same act of surrender we are decreasing the consent for all things and earthly events to enter our life and come out. No matter what unfortunate events appear to be on the horizon of our life, what is substantial is how we react to them. This is the difference between the common man and the one who has awakened.

To the extent that we accept and tolerate all the external actions that influence our existence, we take away the weight of pain and suffering that could arise in me. This does not mean giving up my dreams, but rather not striving to achieve the aims in the sense of resisting everything that opposes. It is to accommodate to the multiple opportunities that arise in the way of adaptation and to arrive at my goal by means other than the one I had expected.

It is to adjust to the circumstances and choose another route that leads me to the same result or to spectacular outcomes that I had not planned, because that is the wisdom of acceptance and letting everything flow. The universe always compensates to a greater degree those who act in order to turn their dreams into realities.

The devotee, who surrenders to his divinity or before the image that represents the divinity, enters a state of trance where there are no problems but solutions. The importance given to the subject matter of concern disappears. Everything else becomes secondary and the only thing that gleams is the presence of the Self or inner divinity that appeases and heals everything.

After deep prayer or meditation I can say: I surrender, I surrender, I surrender to (Jesus, God, and the Divine Energy) and it is as if I transfer my pains and worries to another entity.

Reality is Change.

When we live our micro world, be it family, professional or social, we perceive the nature of change. That is why when we leave our family, we change jobs or settle in another city or country; we fear the future and the events ahead because apparently we have no control over our life. But what if we accepted everything as if it had been our decision? At the bottom of the question, it is the ego that suffers by not satisfying its caprices. Once we learn to separate the ego from our real identity everything flows harmoniously and smoothly because reality is permanent change and transformation.

Do not resist.

The constant of life is change. Humans are accustomed to living in an area where there are no substantial alterations in the coming of existence because we panic. But if nothing is static, even the earth is in permanent movement and fluctuation, why would our discourse be exempt from them? If something produces psychic, mental and even physical wear, it is the opposition or resistance to changes. It is perhaps the number one cause of sorrow and pain. We become infatuated with a given situation, person or object and if they change or disappear we enter the painful nostalgia of loss.

The great masters advice is to let ourselves be carried by the river of existence without opposing the changes and alterations that occur in the normal course of its journey. Learning to eliminate resistance to ups and downs and transformations is one of the secrets to maintaining joviality and happiness of living.accustomed

The key to not resisting is to let everything flow and accommodate to variations. Only the universe in its infinite wisdom confirms that the modifications that occur are positive for us. Otherwise if the apparent changes are painful there is a lesson in spiritual growth that lies behind these experiences. If we learn to experience being, even in the worst of circumstances, we will be calm and happy.

Acceptance and Tolerance.

In addition to eliminating resistance, there is another mantra that will enrich our reality: acceptance and tolerance to everything that happens in the daily course. It means to accommodate my goals and objectives to events with my consent. It is useless to fight against the current of life, at least to maintain permanent mental health and satisfaction. Acceptance and tolerance means blessing the changes because if they did not exist the caterpillar would not become a butterfly. The metamorphosis is then understood as something consubstantial and inherent to one's existence. Acceptance and tolerance for transformation is also a way to save energy that is used to maintain a status quo doomed to disappear. Why fight to continue on our side with a partner that generates dissatisfaction, frustration and grief for fear of the pain of separation? Life demands a modification, without hatred or resentment, without doing any harm, without guilt or remorse. Acceptance and tolerance for change is the healthiest thing in these cases, even for our companion.

Eliminating resistance with acceptance and tolerance situates us within the vibrating universal energy, away from our manipulative and controlling ego. We begin to vibrate in the frequency of our infinite being in contrast to the stubborn and obstinate ego that orbits in a microcosm of pain and dissatisfaction. By pulsating with infinity, we expand the range of our probabilities and feel the universal love that permeates and penetrates everything.opposition or resistance to changes. It is perhaps the number one cause of sorrow and pain. We become infatuated with

A war against everything and against all.

Have you ever thought how much energy is saved by eliminating the resistance so that everything flows? How many daily battles does it take to accept and tolerate change? Someone asks a favor from another person and hopes to receive it because he is not prepared for a NO. As a consequence, he begins to despise the person who did not want or could not do the favor. So it was not a favor, it was an imperious demand of the person or friend. If I accept and tolerate the negative response I will avoid negative feelings and also the physical and psychic exhaustion that comes with the situation and therefore continue to feel affection for the friend or person who did not meet my request.

The lack of tolerance and acceptance can be applied to the world of ideas and opinions in the religious, political and even fashion, where everyone thinks, acts, and dresses or speaks as he pleases. How many deaths would be avoided if a dictator who governs the fates of a country did not insist on imposing his point of view at gunpoint?

Learning to accept and endure is an imperative for our society to enjoy a healthy and pleasant life. Tolerating the events that occur in my life can be the beginning of unsuspected satisfactions and it is along with eliminating the resistance to change, the key to an ego-free life and therefore with the infinite power of my being or intimate reality that vibrates with the universe.

I am vulnerable, I am fragile, I am weak, I am defenseless.

This instruction is addressed to the ego that is superimposed over my true identity. Recognizing the finitude of the ego and the limitation of its power is a good beginning for surrendering or letting go of the circumstances and worries that overwhelm me daily. As I recognize the futility of the ego, its meager values of which it boasts, I can enter into the realm of the inner divinity.

It takes will and modesty to begin identifying the ego with its pyrrhic battles that keep us tied to the morphed field of earthly vanity. We pride ourselves on our possessions, our money, and educational titles; prizes gained in different spheres of knowledge, sport or fame. We are proud of the journeys made and the countries we have seen; of the beauty of the couples we have had and of the material wealth or academic labels that we have earned.

Before the superficial world of today, to maintain a lean body and young skin is synonymous with aesthetics. The cult of the body far surpasses the growth of the soul in terms of solidarity, compassion or love for the underprivileged. To appear in the media is a privilege that many humans seek as a reward for their demagogic efforts to overcome.

The new scientific discoveries, the high technology that should be at the service of humanity to eliminate hunger or give equal opportunities of education is used to keep the human more attached like a pervasive buyer, a slave of consumerism.

Fame, wealth and power are ephemeral forms that enlarge the ego to feel even more separated from the rest of humans in a rictus of superiority over others. But nothing is eternal, except the Being. Everything crumbles like a mountain of snow in the presence of the scorching sun. The absence of material goods or fame causes suffering, nostalgia and pain. All conquests of the ego are trivial, temporary; they are like air that inflates and uproots the individual from his contact with reality. At the end of life when we make a balance sheet of our passage through the planet, how much do economic and social gains weigh compared with internal growth? What produces real satisfaction; accumulating money and disease or eliminating forever all kinds of hatred and traumas of the psyche? Of course it is possible to grow in the plane of life with its riches and attractions and evolve in the character to achieve permanent and constant happiness. But some humans spend all their body energies to obtain immense fortunes and at the end of their life this wealth does not serve them to recover health and the fullness lost.

Beyond the Third dimension.

To feel vulnerable is to recognize that we are not merely this body, but a manifestation of the energy that we are. It is to understand that there are dimensions and worlds with other realities beyond what we can grasp with our 5 senses. This does not mean suppressing desire as an internal force impelling action. It means that when our desires are not satisfied, we do not enter into depression or pain because we intuitively know there is a very powerful inner force that fills us with satisfaction above the earthly desires that are last of all pleasures for the body.

It also means that entering into the neutrality of the Being is to experience pleasure beyond the mundane and that the deficiencies in the material plane can be compensated for by that feeling of immanent love that springs from within. In moments of sadness, it is more effective to do an introspection or meditation that connects us with the depth of being that underlies our conscience than to go for example, shopping. And it is more cost-effective.

Experiencing the vulnerability of the ego is not denying the body. It is recognizing the limitations of the physical and entering into the unlimited power and strength of the inner Self. The true spiritual guide resides in this truth: to discover the influence and inner power of universal love, that is, our own light, without claiming anything in return. If churches were not committed to receiving tithes and taxes they would have real credibility as messengers of love. Because service and compassion for others, pay for themselves. There is no greater pleasure for the soul than to serve. Some hierarchs of the churches are authentic messengers of unconditional love, but they are a minority. That is why today spirituality is shared beyond religions. Jesus urged us to discover our own divinity through love and to share that love with humanity. We are all made in the image and likeness of Divinity and possess the inner divine spark.

Understanding the weakness and vulnerability of the ego over technological advancements or economic conquests is a very useful tool for awakening the inner Divine Being and enjoying the ineffable pleasures of the spirit. Vulnerability is an elementary step to surrender to the power and inner control of universal love. The pleasure of the senses is ephemeral; the joys of the soul are permanent. Worldly pleasure annoys, spiritual bliss pervades all things and connects you with the whole.

Everything matters nothing to me.

In experiencing the divinity within, the clouds in my life disappear. It is a state of total irresponsibility that frees me from my problems. The intensity or weight of such topics is nothing. I disconnect from the construction with my ego that carries those bulks. I disclaim obligations or duties in order to feel the freedom of the individual being that moves in space devoid of time. I float regardless of the results of my inaction. In a simple way I delete the importance of the facts and circumstances by the priority and transcendence of Being or inaction. It is the independence of circumstances, duties, deadlines and commitments. It is the true liberation of the existential anguish, of the necessity of being always tied to the matrix of production and consumption. It is the experience and inner rapture that allow me to be contingent or primordial.

Everything else, even the instinct for survival, disappears. Then I am pure energy

ELIMINATION OF MIND AND EGO WITH KRYON

I eliminate thoughts, feelings and emotions to be in the now. I am in contact with the earth. *Aris.* From my *Omega-Chakra* I make contact with Lady Gaia. *Aris.*

Mind in the *Heart-Chakra.* I imagine a sphere of light. *Heart-Chakra.*

My intention is to suppress the mind. *Shi'a'drana. My* intention is to suppress the ego. *Shi'a'drana.* My intention is to live in the present. *Shi'a'drana.* Mind in the heart. Strength of life. *Pradna.* I am here now, in the absolute present.

Prana. Mind in the *Heart-Chakra.* Here and now pure feelings, pure emotions. *Atrana.* Mind in the sphere of the heart. Pure thoughts here and now. *Mohara.* Mind in the sphere of love. I remove attachments to things, places, pets and people. I erase all my accessories. *Nion.* I remove resisting what happens in my life. *EloO.* I suppress resisting in my work. *Eloo.* I delete resisting in my emotional relationships. *Eloo.* I eliminate resisting the events in my country and the world. *Eloo.* Mind in the the *Heart-Chakra.* I delete the mind that generates fear and pain. *Lotus.* I suppress anarchic thoughts. *Har'Atora.* I delete evoking negative emotions. *El'Gotsha.* I eradicate evoking negative feelings. *Donadas.* I suppress fighting. *Avatara.* I remove aggressiveness. *Tarados.* I delete defending myself from others. *Har'Atora*. Mind in the sphere of light. I eliminate identifying myself with my achievements. I eliminate identifying myself with my belongings. *El'Gotsha*.

I remove identifying myself with fame. *Savier*. I erase identifying myself with power. *Savier*. Acceptance and tolerance. *Hanar*. Acceptance and patience. *Ena*. Mind in the heart. I break down the barrier of resistance. *Eloo*. I am weak, I am defenseless, I am fragile, I am vulnerable. *Savier*. I am weak, I am fragile, I am defenseless, I am vulnerable. *Ena*. Mind in the sphere of light. I give up, I surrender, I surrender to the energy of Jesus Christ. *Ekta*. I give up, I surrender humbly before Shakti and the energy of the masters of light. *Siron*. I agree to lose, I give up, I surrender to Melek Metatron. *Noris*. Mind in the sphere of love. I give myself to the divine energy of Jesus Christ, Buddha and avatars. *Jawes*. I surrender to the divine energy of Jesus. *Ekta*. I surrender myself with all aspects of my body of light to the divine energy. *Ena*. Mind in the heart-Chakra I remove the borders of my being. *Analotus*. I eliminate thoughts, feelings and emotions to be present-now. *Nektum*. I am one with the divine energy of all universes. *El'nora*. I am one with the energy of the divine source of all that is. *Analotus*. Mind in the sphere of light. Energy of being within me. *Sadna*. Energy of the infinite being. *Elexier*. I burst into supreme joy. *Shimaa*. Mind in the heart. Peace and tranquility of Being. *Tarados*. Stillness and calmness of being. *Onar. Mind* in the heart. Joy of Being. *Tanatara*. Happiness of Being. Mind in the *Heart-Chakra*. Supreme Bliss of Being. *Lay'o'esha*. Heart. Infinite Enjoyment of Being. *Lay'o'esha*. Orgasmic energy of love. *Elexier*. Ecstasy of the infinite Being. *Serus*. Unity with all that Is. *El'noras* Ecstasy of the infinite being. *Devar*. The footprint of God. *Shimaa*. Mind in the love- Chakra. Being full of *Nubi* love. Heart. *Lay'o'esha*. Divine energy within me. *Serus*. Mind in the heart. I am everything, I am nothing. *Ena*. I love myself deeply. *Sol'a'vana*. I love myself wholeheartedly. *Nubi*. I am everything, I am nothing. *Rada-soam*, heart. I remove the barrier of containment so that the avalanche of being floods me. *Nektum. Devar.* Divine magic. Catharsis of irrepressible love. *Eschata.* I love myself in all circumstances. I love every aspect of my body of light. I love everyone. *Sol'a'vana.* Ecstasy of the infinite Being. *Kodoish, kodoish, kodoish, Adonai tsebayoth.* Consciousness in the heart.

HOW TO BE IN THE PRESENT- NOW

I suppress my perception of past and future.

I concentrate my mind on the eternal present.

I feel the happiness that emanates from my infinite being when I am in the present.

All my physical senses, my intuition and my wisdom are aligned with my infinite being.

I use all my senses, my intuition and my wisdom free of prejudice. I transform all the fears of my past into wisdom and energy for the present.

If some unconscious fears persist, I will heal them with Gamma-Energetics.

I eliminate anxiety about the results of my future.

I eliminate the depression and sadness of my past to live the joy of the infinite present.

Time is mental, I accustom my mind to live the present.

I cancel from my mind the past and the future so I can live in the now.

I transform all the fears and anxieties of my future into energy to live the present-now.

I remove time control from my routine.

I eliminate the anxiety produced by the control of time.

My work is a meditation on the absolute present.

I am a witness to the thoughts that go around my mind.

I suppress thoughts, feelings and emotions to be in the present, in the pleasant presence of being.

I cast off the energies that draw me out of my present.

I eliminate the haste and the anxiety to perform my daily tasks.

I overpower my eagerness in my daily activities.

I enjoy being aware of my daily work.

When I go around my tasks I suppress thoughts, emotions or feelings that distract me.

I eliminate the negative emotions in my work coming from a reactive boss.

I work with joy at a pleasant and effective pace.

I suppress the negative emotions of my mind coming from facts outside of my work.

I remove the desperation to achieve results or goals.

I focus on one activity at a time.

In the development of my work I suppress time as a preponderant factor.

I focus my awareness on the fundamental things of my work.

My job is fun, full of positive emotions and satisfaction.

I suppress the stress of time.

I am aware of my activity now.

I cancel rambling off in the past or the future.

I transfer my desires and yearnings to my super conscious mind for their crystallization.

My super conscious mind is always connected to my infinite self.

My infinite self is always connected to the Great Spirit or Divine Source of all that Is.

I deliver all my projects to my super conscious mind.

I think from my heart to be in the present-now.

I strive to feel my infinite self in my center-heart in order to be in the now.

To live from the heart is to eliminate the perception of a dual world to be in the now.

I remove my obsessions to stay in the now.

I eliminate all the structures and mental models that prevent me from living in the now.

By living the now I feel my connection with the Divine Source of all that Is.

I am a divine being that inhabits a human body.

Past, present and future occur simultaneously in the absolute present.

To live the present is to be aware of the infinite being within me.

The past and the future are an illusion of the mind. I learn to lead my mind through the eternal present.

I ask the universe that my mind stays always in the present.

I bring the mastery of the present to my life.

I have eliminated all resistance to live in the present- now.

I project in others wisdom, knowledge and happiness that flow from the absolute present within me.

I detach myself from all those habits of evoking the past or straining because of the future.

My attention is always focused in the present-now.

My thoughts, feelings, emotions and beliefs flow in a way that the present- now will arise in my mind.

Through my breathing I am always in the present.

My main goal is to be in the present-now in the realization of my infinite being.

My intention is to think from my center-heart to be always in the now in the supreme realization of being.

My prosperity is born from the absolute present in my mind.

From the present in my mind I manifest all the reality that I desire.

My present from my center-heart generates an integral and successful life on this level

Living the present gives me the necessary balance to satisfy my life and help others.

I assume the responsibility of living my life from the absolute present.

I affirm myself as a master who knows how to live from the present.

I ask the universe to allow me to always be in the present-now.

In my meditations I am always in the now.

I choose today to always be with my mind in the here-now.

I am always, and feel the divine presence within me, in the present-now.

I always vibrate in the frequency of universal love.

When I am in the now, wonderful miracles happen in my life.

I am energy, I am light and love.

When I am present, the purity of my soul clears all my bodies of dense and low-frequency energies.

Everything in this life is perfect and looks perfect from my present-now.

I appreciate everything that comes into my life. I am grateful to be always in the present.

I bless all the events of my life and enjoy them from the present.

I am what I see in others. I strive to see inner divinity and universal love in all beings.

With my verb I command to be all my life immersed in the present-now, far from thoughts, feelings, emotions and beliefs in order to live the infinite being within me.

My faith in my divine being within me allows me to always be in the present now.

I feel the divine grace poured out on my facets, when I am present- now.

When I am present, I am part of the whole and I feel united to the energy of universal love.

I am the power and the glory of the Divine source.

HOW TO BALANCE LIFE

I remove the need to show others what I am capable of.

I vibrate with the infinite being within me.

Being connected to the infinite being makes me powerful.

My connection with self makes me the creator of the greatest achievements.

I avoid competing with others to avoid feeling superior or inferior to anyone.

I believe in myself and the infinite being within me.

My main goal is to realize the infinite being.

I deserve all the abundance and wealth of this life.

I attract all the abundance and wealth.

My happiness is within me, in the fulfillment of my being.

All the goals that I propose in this life, I make them come true.

I eliminate all the sins that enter my psyche.

I deserve all the honors and admiration of others.

I have the ability to struggle to achieve my goals.

Money comes into my life with grace and ease.

I feel beautiful. I am beautiful.

I eliminate all programs that limit me in the expression of myself being infinite.

I am a loving, compassionate and kind person.

I erase from my psyche all criticism programs

I am the most intelligent being. I am a genius.

I am the bravest and the noblest.

I have absolute confidence in my mental, physical and spiritual capacities.

I am protected by my angels and beings of light.

I am indifferent to the criticism of others.

I suppress judging others.

I eliminate criticizing others.

I delete blaming others.

I remove punishing others.

I eliminate sentencing others.

Everything comes to my life with ease.

I attract and enjoy the earthly successes without neglecting my spiritual path.

I feel satisfied and fulfilled.

In difficult circumstances, the strength of my infinite being emerges.

I am always optimistic by nature.

I remove the fear of the future.

I always live in the present and I enjoy it to the fullest.

I am very happy. I feel the supreme bliss of being within me.

I do all my tasks with ease and enjoyment.

I avoid comparing myself to others.

I eliminate the observance of others in my work.

I am confident of the maximum quality of my work.

I refuse to criticize myself.

I welcome the jokes and mockery of others.

I suppress all beliefs that restrict or impede my freedom.

I integrate easily with social groups.

I remove all the programs that limit me.

I feel very confident of my talents and I thank God for possessing them.

I live in communion with the infinite being.

I live in divine grace.

I am at the service of others.

I am aware of the pleasure-pain duality and try to remain in the divinity of being.

I delete showing others what I am capable of.

All the supposed limitations of the human are in duality.

All the powers of the human are in the enjoyment of the infinite being within.

I am capable, if I will, of the greatest feats.

I am an unlimited being of strength and love.

I am the expression of aesthetics, universal love and divine power.

I am an unlimited being full of abilities and potentialities.

I am the expression of pure freedom.

I esteem my freedom as a component of my happiness and fulfillment.

I vibrate in unity with everything.

SILENCE THE MIND FROM THE HEART

An effective way to silence the mind of your inane wandering is to locate the consciousness in the heart-chakra, where the power of divinity resides. According to the HeartMath Institute, the magnetic field of the heart is 5,000 times stronger than the magnetic field generated in the human brain. So if we want to stay in the now, it is easier to concentrate that energy in the heart-chakra or spiritual heart where all the energies of Being come together.

Once I have centered my consciousness on the spiritual heart, I give the order to my mind to remain in the now, in the absolute present guided by the powerful magnetic field of the heart. If the mind wants to ramble, I simply focus my consciousness on the spiritual heart and give the command to stay in the now.

All the activity is centered in the spiritual heart, so I live all the experiences from there and that way I guarantee to be always focused on the here-now. The following prayers or instructions help me to keep myself in the present free from the absurd drifts of the mind:

Think with the heart.

Live from the heart.

Watch, and be a witness from the heart.

Feel from the heart.

Perceive everything from the heart.

Assent time from the heart.

Live in the present from the heart.

Be thankful from the heart.

Have the intention of transferring mental activity to the heart.

Reason and aim from the heart.

Harmonize experience from the heart.

Raise the vibration and frequency of my being from the heart.

Organize all thoughts from the heart.

Understand the unity from the heart. Nothing is right or false from it. From my heart nothing is good or bad.

I connect my brain to my heart.

All my decisions are full of love. All my judgments are full of love.

My heart regulates my life. I raise my consciousness, my light and my energy from my heart.

I decree to always think and act from my heart.

You can practice daily by repeating each instruction during waking time to keep your mind always under control.

I think from my heart -chakra.

I live integrated to the powerful force of my heart field.

I watch events from the heart. My heart is a fair and thoughtful witness of becoming.

I perceive life from my center heart in my chest.

I feel how everything flows from the equanimity of my center- heart.

Time from my heart is now sacred.

I am thankful for everything that happens in my life from my spiritual heart.

My mind is always connected to my center-heart in every circumstance.

My analysis and reasoning arise from the state of being in my heart-chakra.

All the experiences harmonize with the energy and frequency that my spiritual heart emits.

By connecting with my center heart, I raise both the frequency and vibration of my consciousness to be in the infinite being.

All thoughts are controlled by my being in the spiritual heart.

I feel the unity in love with all beings from my center heart.

Nothing is false or true from my center heart.

Nothing is good or bad.

Nothing is beautiful or unpleasant.

No one is intelligent or of limited intellect.

From my spiritual heart all extremes or opposites end. Everything in a simple way is.

My brain is always connected to the brain of my heart.

All my decisions are filled with love from the infinite being residing in my center- heart

All my judgments are full of love and respect.

I remove qualifying circumstances, decisions, things, the environment, animals or people.

The being that inhabits my center heart regulates my life.

A radiant sun of light, love and happiness flashes from my center -heart.

I am aware of my breathing and focus my attention on the heart-chakra as I breathe.

The pure Lord who invades the atom and the space of the cosmos springs forth from the depths of my spiritual heart.

My inner world is full of love, compassion, mercy and happiness.

I am an unlimited being full of possibilities when I direct my destiny from my center-heart.

I ask to be always centered in my spiritual heart.

I constantly resonate with the energies of the highest evolution and frequencies.

I erase the resistance to daily happenings and to always vibrate in the infinite being that lives in my center-heart.

My whole existence is a reflection of the infinite being that resides in my spiritual heart.

I project pure love to everything that surrounds me.

My freedom is born from total detachment for the mundane that is entrenched in my center-heart where the being shines immanent.

My attention is focused on always living in the heart and from the spiritual heart.

From my heart I observe how the vital river flows and everything changes.

I am prosperous and abundant without losing my life's quality which gives me awakening and enlightenment. These nourish themselves with the energy that springs from my center-heart.

My strong desire is to be awake and illuminated with the vibrations emitted by my spiritual heart.

My supreme intention is to abide in the infinite being, where delights are awaiting in my spiritual heart.

I think and act from my spiritual heart to turn this journey on earth into paradise.

From my spiritual heart I manifest all the events that accompany my path in life.

All my actions are born from love and compassion.

I decide in this life to undertake all the learning and knowledge I need for evolving.

I am responsible for all of my actions and always decide from my center-heart in the calmness of being.

My intuition is a force that comes from my heart and guides me in the most delicate decisions.

I am an ascended, awakened and enlightened being.

My meditations are aimed at strengthening the settlement of my consciousness in the heart-chakra, the entrance to my soul.

All my decisions are aimed at uniting love and compassion with everything around me.

I eliminate fear, envy, rejection, resentment, guilt and attachment so that the high vibration and the frequency of pure and universal love shine forth in my heart.

The most precious miracle of this life is to be immersed in the ocean of goodness, beauty and universal love of the infinite being within me

My true balance and strength are found in the pureness of the divine being that governs my actions.

The brilliant energy coming from my heart–chakra cleanses my surroundings.

I breathe in the sacred now from my heart-chakra. *Ananasha*.

Kodoish, kodoish, kodoish. Adonai tsebayot.

I command the aligning of my thoughts, feelings, emotions and beliefs to my center-heart, the epicenter of love.

I have faith in acting and coexisting with the most beautiful feelings and emotions to influence the river of survival.

Divine grace, joy and glory are the sap that comes from my spiritual heart and permeates all my actions.

From my heart I embrace unity in love with all that is.

EXPERIENCE THE DIVINITY

After bending the ego, our true identity emerges as when the veil of ignorance unfurls a blazing sun. Concentrating attention on the heart-chakra and feeling pleasure and love for all things appears swiftly from the center of our being, like an overwhelming and irresistible feeling that escapes as if it were repressed for a long time. It is a feeling of total freedom to be integrated into all things. From within comes unspeakable happiness that permeates the surrounding universe. The floodgates of the Being are opened and we receive the avalanche of irrepressible love that permeates everything.

It is a pure love that escapes from the center-heart in the Chakra of the same name and runs in all directions. In particular, we feel an unequaled pleasure when this energy flows through our back and shines around in 360 degrees like a glorious sun. Then a new vibration explodes full of strength and power. It is the imprint of the most precious energy: the footprint of God.

All our concerns turn banal in the face of this majestic portal of inner energy. We are then connected to all beings and to all things through this incomprehensible love. All earthly goals seem to come together here, the subtlest aspect of the mighty existence. There are no sensations that can be compared to the immense happiness that springs like a fountain from the bottom of the center-heart. It is the joy, the happiness, the supreme delight of the Being. It is the immortal paradise that resides within an unsuspected brilliance. It is the dimension of the now, devoid of space and time. It is the perennial comfort for all the sufferings of body and soul. It is the heavenly balm that relieves the pain born of earthly attachments.

Suddenly we feel the connection with the universes. From a limited and finite heart explodes the creative power that vibrates in the frequency of the infinite Being that connects us with all forms.

It is the unlimited universal consciousness that communicates us with all the great hearts of this and other galaxies, because pure love is the universal language of beings that have evolved in all dimensions.

Keeping those pleasure-seeking sensations of the spirit is now our will. To remain immersed in that ecstasy of the soul as if we were never to experience it again is our priority. To live immersed in that pleasurable and orgasmic force of Being. It is paradise on earth. The ultimate alchemy of life that resides in the lowest point of our existence, beyond the ego.

The unlimited power of being (solitude).

The ruling being that governs my heart is unlimited.

The powers of my being are infinite.

My being is connected to the divine source of all that is.

My Divine being rules my cells.

Every cell of the 144 billion that inhabit my body receives orders from my being.

I am a powerful, merciful and loving being.

Through universal love my cells connect with all beings that inhabit this planet and also beings of other dimensions.

To nourish myself I need only the light and love that emanates from me to be Divine.

I can heal all people by contacting love and the infinite power of my divine Being.

All the elements that my body requires to be younger and more vigorous, spring forth from my divine being contained in my heart- chakra.

From the center of my being I am the divine spark that penetrates everything.

I am immanent light and truth.

I communicate with all existences from my divine self to theirs, being latent or active.

I am the vital or flat energy that dwells in everything.

I travel through galaxies in the company and with the breath of my divine being.

My divine being in its pure essence, modifies matter

In my healings I respect the karma that others must fulfill.

The purpose in this life is to know and enjoy the divine being.

I refuse to resist events for my being to shine.

My ego submits first, so that the infinite presence of the Being appears.

I eradicate the offenses received, to have the right of reason, fame, identifying myself with wealth and the need to win so that the grandeur of the Being in me appears flawless.

The emptiness of the atom and space are filled with divine prana, the essence of my Being.

I eliminate identifying myself with my body, in order to feel all aspects of my merkaba, the strength and energy of Being.

I serve everyone from my divine Being.

My being increases with service, mercy, tolerance and love for others.

I feel the completeness of my soul and all aspects of my body of light.

Being in the now, I welcome the powerful energy of other planes of existence

I am full of divine grace that is irrigated in all the cells of my body.

Divine purity invades all my bodies.

I share the beautiful energy of creating other life planes.

I live to forgive all offenses and to love without measure.

I have made the decision to live always connected to my divinity, in all the actions of each day.

In my actions and in my voice I show the inner harmony of the Being.

Awakening in my Self is the most precious gift of all my lives.

By living in the Being I feel total detachment for all things mundane. I admire the pristine beauty of this world and the pleasures that it holds, but I separate myself from all addictions.

By remaining in the presence of the Being in the now, in the divine emancipation of my center-heart, I experience peace, quiet, confidence and security before all avatars of life.

I live, I experience, I feel, I perceive Sol'A'Vana, the presence of God, the inheritance of God, the breath of God.

Purity of being. Nasha'o.

I am the power and glory of the divine source.

All these instructions are recorded in the water element of my body for its transformation and health.

MONEY AS ENERGY

I deserve to receive money in abundance from the universe.

I am willing to receive the money to fulfill the purposes of my life.

I choose to receive money in abundance with the purpose of achieving the goals and objectives of my life and to serve others.

I overturn the fear of receiving money in abundance.

I suppress criticizing the rich.

I delete judging the rich.

I eliminate blaming the rich.

I remove from my cells envying the rich.

I eliminate hating the rich and successful people.

I remove all obstacles to receive money, easily and without causing harm to anyone.

I suppress all negative judgments in relation to money.

I eliminate my anxiety and worries about money.

I receive all the energy vibrations that connect me with money and abundance.

I ask from the universe access to wealth and abundance.

I use the media to promote what I do or sell.

I delete all doubts regarding receiving money and wealth.

I imagine my life with abundance and wealth. I imagine all the things I can obtain and the activities I can do with wealth. (Pause for several minutes to let the imagination fly and visualize concrete things that I desire and activities related to abundance and wealth).

I specifically imagine the objects and things I can get with those means. (Pause to imagine the enjoyment of them).

I believe in my abilities and mental strength to create money for myself.

I eliminate all the mental structures and models of this and other lives that prevent me from getting money.

I eliminate the fear of wealth.

Of all the possibilities I choose, I select those that are the most useful to generate me wealth.

Money comes into my life with ease, joy and abundance.

I work on what I enjoy and also earn money.

I remove the belief that lack and poverty are key to spiritual development.

Using the right media to offer my services or products makes it easier to earn money.

I suppress the programs or instructions that invite me to reject money.

I always collect money for my services or products because I deserve it.

I accept all the gifts of the universe.

I refuse to cling to money and wealth.

I remove from my cells the program: 'money is sin'. I erase the guilt that implies such thinking.

The Infinite being is power and abundance to serve with humility.

I eradicate all structures, patterns or mental models of this or other lives that prevent me from receiving from the universe.

With my thoughts I build the way to be abundant and rich.

I erase the fear of wealth.

I take away from my cells the fear of penalty for being abundant and rich.

I prepare myself to manage economic success and wealth.

I have faith in my present-now and fill it with abundance and wealth.

I smooth the way and prepare myself to receive money in abundance without harming or hurting others.

I delete the religious belief that being poor is the way to reach heaven. I reach that when I feel the infinite being within me.

I use abundance and wealth to serve others.

I erase from my cells the program that says: 'It is easier for a camel to go through the eye of a needle than for a rich man to enter the kingdom of heaven'.

I eliminate all the poverty of my psyche in particular the lack of spirit and heart.

I deserve abundance and wealth to serve myself and help others.

I choose not to hoard money out of avarice or greed.

I erase stinginess from my cells. Money must flow and move around because it is energy.

I share with the needy and let the money that comes into my life flow freely.

I always save a percentage of my income.

I erase scarcity from my cells.

I avoid people who complain about lack and poverty.

I am confident, positive and optimistic in relation to receiving money from the universe through people.

The universe provides me easily with abundance and wealth without anxiety or struggle to obtain them.

I eliminate manipulating others in order to get money.

Money comes from my work, from business that I create and from the divine will that wishes so.

I choose lucrative activities with respect towards morals and ethics. I make money without causing damage to others.

I remove the instruction 'Blessed are the poor because of them is the kingdom of heaven'

The kingdom of the heavens has settled in me, in my Heart- Chakra.

I eliminate the program 'money is sin' with which I have been manipulated in the past.

I am always connected to the divine source and as such I provide everything I need for my evolution.

I invest the surplus of my income into profitable goods with respect toward ethics.

I always save to face eventualities.

I search for activities that profit me and generate money, with adherence to ethics and morals.

I prepare myself intellectually with a profession that allows me to increase my income.

Unless my income is plentiful, I avoid getting in debt, high interest rates or usury because I would be working for lenders.

If I have abundant income I can use cheap credit to expand my means of work.

My expenses are always less than my income.

I avoid the unnecessary and irresponsible expenses that prevent me from saving.

I center my attention on the infinite being within me that gives me all the spiritual happiness that I deserve.

I prefer a simple and authentic life to the unreal and superfluous one that creates envy and hatred.

I suppress the need of buying unnecessary goods just because they are on sale.

I live according to my income in the happiness of my being.

I feel genuine happiness in helping others.

I use cash to buy and save the discounts given by doing so.

I avoid borrowing money needlessly for buying unnecessary things.

I am optimistic. My income grows exponentially.

I deserve abundance.

Real poverty is the poverty of spirit and heart.

I start my jobs or business with enthusiasm and happiness.

I repeat every day to myself 'I am wealthy, I am abundant.

I avoid superfluous expenses for appearances or snobbery.

I am an infinite being who creates abundance and wealth without moving away from my goal which is enlightenment.

I avoid rejecting the gifts that the universe gives me through others

I feel comfortable receiving.

I erase all the guilty structures of this and other lives that prevent me from enjoying wealth and abundance.

Money like any energy must flow, it needs to come and go.

I ask of the universe support for the projects that will make me abundant and prosperous.

I eliminate the resistance to be prosperous

I reflect success, with balance, prosperity and wealth.

I Project in others prosperity.

I detach myself from all wealth and riches of this world

I let the money flow at its own pace.

I am generous and abundant.

My goal is to be successful in my family relationships, spiritual development, solidarity with others, hobbies and my prosperity.

I think, speak and act as a prosperous being without putting aside the priority of my infinite being.

I reflect and manifest my own reality full of success in professional and spiritual prosperity.

I am successful for the balanced development of the material and spiritual areas in my life's path.

I assume prosperity with responsibility.

I affirm myself as a being of light, accepting abundance and prosperity from the universe.

My prayers are directed toward my realization and enlightenment as a helpful human.

In my meditations I center myself in the being that is abundant and generous.

I choose all paths that will lead me to enlightenment without rejecting abundance.

I vibrate in the frequency of pure love which creates peace, harmony, abundance, kindness, compassion and generosity.

I seek a righteous existence to reach my own divinity.

I am energy of pure love that fills my cells with health, abundance and kindness.

I purify my life by doing well to others.

I am grateful to the universe for abundance and prosperity which I humbly receive without offending others.

With the power of my word, I decree forever to be abundant and prosperous without undermining my spiritual goals which are the enlightenment and realization of the divine being.

I have faith in fulfilling my plans to always live in the infinite being.

I receive divine grace with humility.

I remove my ego and so of others in order to enjoy the divine energy that mingles in all beings.

THE PURITY AND DIVINESS OF SEX

I change the conception of 'sex is sin' for:

I eliminate feeling guilty in order to enjoy sex.

I remove the taboo associated with sexual activity or social prohibition of sex.

Sex is a sublime way of contacting the divinity in me.

Sex is sacred.

I always procure to have safe sex. I expel entities that could enter my electromagnetic field as a result of a sexual relationship.

Orgasm is a connection with the Divine in me.

I endeavor to have a steady partner.

When possible I try not to waste my seeds, fruit of a sexual relationship.

As I meditate during sexual intercourse, I awaken my *kundalini*.

I emigrate from the morphed field of aberration and sexual guilt.

I get rid of the morbid and pornographic connotations in my sexual relations to feel the connection with my infinite being.

I feel an infinite love for my partner during intercourse.

Sexual satisfaction inhibits me from sins, guilt's and errors.

Sex with spiritual love is the ultimate happiness on this level.

In my sexual relationship, I always seek the happiness and satisfaction of my partner.

Sex accompanied by universal and spiritual love is an initiation in spiritual awakening.

I always ask my partner first to authorize any sexual game.

The main interest that motivates me in a sexual relationship is to achieve spiritual fulfillment through the satisfaction and happiness of myself and my partner.

Sexual orgasm is a connection with the purity of my being.

Orgasm makes me vibrate in the frequency of the Divine Source of all that Is.

I eliminate selfishness from my sexual relations. I always seek the satisfaction of my partner and my own.

The purpose of sexual intercourse is the union of two spirits and two bodies to attain divine glory.

Sexual intercourse is of divine origin.

I remove all the sins and guilt's associated with sexual satisfaction.

I suppress the original sin from my cells.

The sexual energy produced by two souls who love each other generates the greatest miracles.

The energy produced by two souls which are in love in a sexual relationship, fills the energetic reserves of each lover in a positive way.

I make sure every sexual relationship is a meditation to become a superior human being.

In every sexual relationship I feel the purity and splendor of both my soul and my lover's.

In my sexual relationships I combine the purity of my thoughts, feelings and emotions with sexual play.

Sex is pure, clean and the expression of universal love.

I eliminate attachment and love which brings pain in my sexual relationships.

I suppress affection for sex that generates addiction.

I refuse to mistreat or be mistreated in my sexual relations.

I feel the Divine presence in my sexual relations.

Sex is the greatest gift of love in this life.

I cast out from my psyche all forms of pain in my sexual relations.

I reject physical or emotional discomfort in my sexual relationships.

I reject all sexual practice devoid of love, tenderness, sweetness and the noblest feelings.

I eliminate from my mind the models and structures that inhibit me to enjoy the purity of sex.

Sex is a deep and intimate connection with the divine of the human being.

By practicing sex with the highest feelings and emotions of my soul, I connect with God the Creator of All That Is

I am the power and glory of the divine source.

PERCEIVE THE DIVINITY IN THE OTHER

I change my way of perceiving beyond the senses to interpret everything, starting from knowledge and wisdom.

You and I are equal.

I erase from my cells the feeling that I am different from others.

I wipe out the perception of the ego in others, to understand them from divine perfection.

Perfect equivalence between beings occurs when no mind exercises power over the other.

I perceive from my ancestral knowledge and wisdom.

Equality occurs when we exercise the freedom to choose.

Freedom is love.

I free myself from others when I give them freedom.

Others are released from me, when they apply their freedom.

No one can love another imprisoning him.

You and I are united by divine energy

My power is not born of individuality but from energetic union with my fellow men.

It is the energy of blending with all beings that produces miracles.

The supreme energy that binds all things and elements is pure love.

The energy of integration with other humans is greater than the sum of its parts.

Through service I join with all humans in pure love.

It is through the energetic union with all humans how the Great Spirit or divine source of all-that-is is formed.

I send you universal love because of what you are and likewise I receive from you the purity of universal love.

Regardless of race, social position or physical appearance, I always perceive you in the light and harmony of universal love.

I feel the fullness of the power of love when I identify with other humans.

When I see someone I eliminate the differences that come from information of my senses, to perceive and feel the light of love that emerges from its being.

My strength and power are given me when I energetically attach myself to the unique power of pure love that resides in all beings.

When I am free from judgments I can see the Divine in others.

By suppressing my ego, I can unite with you in universal love.

When I free myself from thoughts, feelings and emotions, I can connect with the highest of your energy.

When you free yourself from the ego you can see the best in me.

Union expresses itself as solidarity, compassion and universal love.

I come from union in love with all beings. I return to the same in pure love which is my perennial home.

Our common identity is beyond your ego and mine.

Peace is born when I demolish the illusion of separation with all beings.

By joining with your energy beyond the ego, I remove the fear of feeling the whole.

I dispose any sexual connotation in my approach to your energy of universal love.

I join with others in the intention and desire to serve and to help.

I erase my ego to be able to see you in the splendor of your divinity.

Ego is my false identity, infinite being is my reality.

The reality of the ego is temporary; the divinity is immutable and eternal.

When I live my true reality I feel the glory and happiness in others and myself.

All beings are divine when I look beyond their personal appearance.

I see others beyond their ego, in their true reality.

Through pure love, I erase the fear of others.

I do not seek to change reality; instead I accept it in a humble way.

When I am attacked by others, I discard to blame them to concentrate on keeping my pure love for their infinite being.

I erase the illusion of separation from the divine source in others, to appreciate their effulgent being.

Pure love transmits itself from one infinite being to the other.

Your light is the experience of happiness.

I approach others with humility.

Every human I behold is a Divine being transcending his body; I see it beyond the 3 dimensions in the infinity of its essence.

Pure love is the fifth element like earth, water, air and fire. Pure love is the highest expression of divine energy in the cosmos and in the atom.

I ask the universe to always perceive the divinity in the other.

I resonate with people who see the infinite being beyond and above the 3 dimensional physical information.

I erase the resistance to feeling the infinite being in others.

I reflect impartial love on others.

I focus my mind on discerning divinity in others.

Everything in this life flows allowing the infinite being to be seen in others.

Through perception in others of the infinite being in them, I am able to enjoy enlightenment.

My powerful intention is focused on feeling the infinite being in myself and in others.

I deeply desire to realize the being and to sense it in others.

I firmly believe in myself and have confidence in ascending as a human.

I eliminate being absorbed by duality as I maintain the balance of the infinite being within me.

I work every day on raising my vibration level to eternally perceive the divinity within me and the humans I deal with.

I understand the character of others above their physical appearance, dogmas or customs.

I uphold myself as an ascended and awakened human who is enlightened in pure love.

I request the universe to allow me to feel the infinite being in my heart-chakra and the energy of others.

In my meditation I concentrate in the center-heart in order to feel the divinity present in me and others.

I choose to feel divinity within myself and in other human beings.

I strive to raise my vibration to be able to live always in pure love.

I am a being of light and love that lives in balance with his emotions.

I transmute all thoughts, feelings, emotions and negative beliefs in universal love from my center-heart to heal my bodies.

I purify my environment and my bodies with the essence of pure love that springs forth from my Heart Chakra. I purify my environment and every human that relates to me.

I see the pure essence of the being in you. *Nashaom.*

I change my perspective to always appreciate pure love in other humans.

I am grateful for the elevation of my vibration frequency that allows me to see divinity in others.

I bless with pure love every human who carries the flame of universal love in his heart.

With all the power of my word, I decree to be aware of my infinite being and comprehend that sublime energy in others.

With faith and trust in my infinite being and through yours, we build a new energy for planet earth where harmony reigns

I realize divine grace in you.

Recognizing your divinity brings us both to unity in pure love. The divine source is one, and we all are the divine source of everything that is.

You are the power and glory of the Great Spirit.

You are pure love, pure happiness.

I LOVE MYSELF

I plunge into the sea of energy and light.

To evolve into higher frequencies, I cleanse my soul of all that I no longer need for my transformation.

I love the seed of Jesus Christ and with it I deeply love myself.

I love my soul, I love my spirit.

I see in others the essence of love and compassion.

I treat all beings with love and compassion.

I accept in my soul the change that the Buddha universe requires for my ascension.

Compassion fertilized my psyche to glorify me in happiness.

Love for all beings begins with love for me. To do so I erase all beliefs and programs that distracts my evolution.

Today I breathe to be in the now at all time, in the energy of the infinite being within my heart-chakra where the immense happiness of being and the joy of living reside.

I breathe in the light of love that gushes into my electromagnetic field

I feel an energetic change in all the cells of my bodies.

My heart is moved by the brightness of the light of the soul.

I share all the energy of love with Lady Gaia to whom I owe the sustaining of my 3-dimensional life.

I am united to everything in pure love, a condition inherent in all beings. From my heart emerges the force of love towards me, with respect toward my divinity and with respect and love for others.

I try to remain isolated from the obstinacy for the issues of the future, to be aware of the now.

I transform pain and suffering into immeasurable bliss of the being.

I am the planted seed that receives the indispensable elements to reproduce universal love.

I eliminate identifying with my ego.

I am the supreme bliss residing in the cells of every living organism. I understand that my mind and heart can take me to the last frontier of evolution and transformation in this life by reproducing in me the seed of good.

I seek the transformation of my soul to reach the highest goal of evolution.

I delete painful love for people, things, animals, nature or places.

I transform pleasant and positive emotions into permanent ones, with the consciousness set in emotions and converted into feeling

With pure love I connect with the cosmos to make all thoughts of joy come true: Satisfaction, happiness and harmony.

I remove the habits that give me pain in the duality of consciousness.

I modify the cosmos that surrounds me through altruistic, noble and merciful feelings.

My feelings of pure love are the most powerful tool to build my life and take advantage of it for my own evolution and ascension.

I avoid fighting pain to warn off duality and escape from it.

My meditation and prayers are focused on following my own enlightenment as a human being that clarifies the purpose of life to others.

In this sacred moment I melt into the most sublime energies of the cosmos and the central sun of the galaxy.

A deep feeling of pure love for all that exists is the common denominator of my existence.

I discard all resistance to the events that occur in my life. I fill all succession of facts with the presence of the being.

I have infinite compassion for myself.

I feel pure love for my soul.

In my meditations the intention prevails to realize pure love.

I transform daily thoughts, emotions and beliefs into feelings of pure and universal love

I call upon the hologram which records all thoughts to fill it with pure love and compassion.

By vibrating in pure love for myself, I project love to the universe.

By repeating a noble emotion, I turn it into a divine feeling.

My relationship with myself is full of honesty.

I commune every day with the love of all that exists, in particular the love for me as a component of a multidimensional and infinite being.

The world is a reflection of my transformation as a compassionate being.

I heal all negative emotions in my life so that pure love flows through all the cells of my body.

I quiet my ego. I silence my ego.

I suppress lying to myself.

I trade all the feelings that invite me to suffer such as hatred, anger, revenge, for harmony and peace from my being.

I heal all fears for things to come that torment me, to live in the now in the immensity of the being.

I clean up all the feelings, emotions or beliefs that led me to suffering in the past, and take delight in the present now.

I cast out all expectations produced by worlds of fantasy, to feel the moments of the present- now in the divine presence of the being.

I love the immediacy in my life when the perfect light of the divine shines within me.

The train of my thoughts is running through the labyrinths of now, departing from and arriving to my heart-chakra, my center of love.

The immediacy in my life is filled with love for self above ego, which is the basis of love for others.

The close and nearby events are dependent on my psyche to be what I am.

I am what I am, therefore I exist.

I am infinite love. It is so.

With my first and second thought, I am in the now, in divine grace.

I interrupt all obsessions to perceive the now, here in the simultaneous present.

My heart is the rudder that controls the frenzied journey of my mind through the shameless landscape of suffering and pain.

When I free myself from anger, guilt's and attachments, I access the now in the reflection of the being.

My only alienation is the infinite love within me.

All my ideas converge like a river that surrenders to the sublime ocean of the now.

I open my heart to love all humans, all things and all beings, without measure.

My inner world is perfect, like the splendor created in the exterior by the divine source.

All things are impregnated with love, grace and glory.

I breathe and I exist. I inhale pure love.

With this thought and the former one, I live in the now as a drop containing the eternal sea of happiness.

My heart records the passage of instants, in the supreme rejoicing of the now.

I guide the impermanence of the outside towards the unchanging sweetness of the soul.

My personal group of angels bursts protection and care in the subtleties of mind and time.

My environment is clothed with the everlasting love of eons, centuries, years and the moments of the now.

I am the perfect Light that flashes forth from the sun of suns.

In wandering and journeying in search of elusive happiness, I found it right here in my chest, in the heart-chakra where my infinite being resides; in the labyrinths of the sacred chamber, the door to the soul.

LIVING IN THE BEING

When we insist to be in the absolute present, our interest revolves around finding within each human its divine essence. If you know another way to find your inner Self, you can skip the exercises that lead you to the present-now.

But being in the now is not the end of the journey but a key stage in experiencing the most extraordinary sensation of paradise here on earth, within the mundane noise and the most diverse vibrations that affect your electromagnetic field and your body. It is the way to feel the most beautiful frequencies despite and beyond the various obstacles to be happy. Having achieved the purpose of experiencing the Self, we begin an unlimited journey of powers ranging from the healing of many illnesses and mental or emotional imbalances to the Healing of others based on that wonderful energy that emerges within us. Ensuring an existence full of happiness, health and love is also one of the advantages of living the inner Self.

Being in the present is a tool to lock identification with the ego and worldly events. Experiencing the inner Self controls the vibration and frequency of thoughts so as not to be at the mercy of collective thought waves of the unconscious or low-frequency thoughts. Being in the now and in the being means taking care of the emission of thoughts which are lights to the path of this life. That is, to remain in the high frequencies of universal love, compassion, empathy and desire to serve, contrary to the thoughts of war, hatred, evil, envy, sadness, desolation and fears that most humans automatically transmit.

Select the Media.

To achieve the goal of being away from unhappy thoughts from the past or the frustrating future that the mind drives, select the media you watch or read each day. Note that these means help you in spiritual progress and in learning what you must accomplish here in the school of earth. Avoid stories and news of violence, hatred, revenge, pain and trauma as central themes of what you get. If you cannot help it, be aware that inside you have already cleansed those feelings and emotions from events that occurred in the past and consciously refuse to accept those behaviors that generate more violence and evil.

The variety of information we receive today allows us to select excellent programs that contribute to scientific knowledge and spiritual development. Our electromagnetic field and therefore our mind are influenced by thousands of frequencies of all kinds that permeate the same and incite different actions. A strategy to take into account is to give the command to hate and evil to leave the collective unconscious. Morphed groups exist that transmit information of Healing, of universal and unconditional love; of human solidarity. But also, in most cases, the unconscious information we receive is not the best. Notice that most of the fears you perceive are not yours. Command these frequencies to leave your electromagnetic field and focus your attention on the now or the inner Self. Be aware of all the pernicious influences that inflate your ego and stimulate thoughts of tragedy or emotional pain. Be aware of your body and your breathing to enter into the now.

Focus your mind in the heart-chakra and enjoy its essence, its intimate substance, its true self and the vibrations of happiness that come to your life

with each second that goes by. It is Eden on earth. It is the immutable Being that resides within you, far from the duality of pleasure and pain. It is true happiness free from riches, fame and power. It is the simplicity of life and the genuine flow of the human. A real treasure residing in you.

Energy deficit and disease.

Humans feed on solar energy through plants, water and animals. But the greatest source of energy for the body and other aspects of the *merkaba* is provided by prana or vital energy that is captured in different ways.

When the energy of physical, mental, emotional or spiritual bodies diminishes, we are at risk of producing imbalances in those bodies that later manifest as disease. The most dense and tangible result is physical illness. In a simple way, this can be summarized as an alarm that indicates that emotional, mental or spiritual problems must be healed. We must ensure that the energy we obtain or produce is greater than the energy we consume during physical exercise, work and mental or emotional problems that are connected with our daily activity.

Sleep is one of the highest means to capture energy, when it is profound and refreshing. A well done and conscious abdominal breathing helps us to gather a lot of *prana* or *chi* for daily consumption and helps us to obtain a health-giving sleep, as recommended by the Ramacharaka yogi.

You cannot pretend to holistically heal the human being if you have energy deficit from a lacking night's rest. To obtain *prana* we must practice some aerobic activity, preferably outdoors. We can also do *hatha yoga*, meditation in its many forms; *Chi Kung, chi kung shaolin, falun dafa, tai chi chuan* and develop *pranayama* breathing.

The *sine qua non* condition for healing is to restore the body's energy balance by working less and enjoying more.

The relationship between disease and energy is inversely proportional; to higher energy, less possibility of disease and vice versa; to less amount of energy, greater the possibility for affections and ailments. In pre-modern China all diseases, particularly those of the psyche, were cured with *Chi Kung* or *Tai Chi Chuan*.

Another way to lose energy is that which originates with entities or spirits that adhere to the electromagnetic field of the person for various reasons. The individual is very psychic, that is, goes unconscious in other dimensions or consumes alcohol and loses the notion of his identity or consumes hallucinogenic substances that carry his mind to other dimensions where it loses its autonomy. Under these conditions the entities penetrate the electromagnetic field and are installed permanently until someone can expel them from there.

When using alcohol, hallucinogens and prescribed barbiturates, the individual can enter in stages of pleasurable ecstasy which can last for several hours, but after the production of pleasure hormones ceases, depression or low energy moves in. This energy deficit must be balanced, pushing the person to resort to more alcohol or a drug abuse in order to replace the lost energy and thus begins the vicious circle of consumption. There will come a time when the damage to the body is so severe that even the intake of huge amounts of these substances fails to balance the strength or stamina needed to lead a normal life.

How to receive Prana.

To receive *prana* or *chi*, go to a park if you live in the city or go to the countryside if possible and have a direct contact with nature, which transmits much energy through plants and vegetation. Gently exercise with your mind focused on breathing in a simple way, emphasizing your attention on the abdominal breathing, such as a baby breathes, or your pet. Try to inflate the abdomen with inspiration and deflate it with exhalation. The breathing rate should be slow, sustained and continuous, without effort.

Disconnecting yourself from daily problems eliminates draining energy with thoughts that fuel fears and negativism. Remaining in the present-now in the presence of the Being increases the *Prana* in our bodies.

If nature is not easily available, use meditation every day. It is an effective way to eliminate toxic wastes from the psyche such as anger, envy, emotional pain and fears. By focusing your energy you begin to replenish *prana* lost by activity. The meditation should be done daily, before starting the work routine, preferably before taking a shower. Contemplation is a means of connecting with your real identity. The feelings of love and compassion that emanate from your mental exercise will fill your body cells with *Prana*

If you have enough time, do a daily routine of *Tai Chi* or *Chi Kung*. You can easily find information on the internet regarding this matter. *Falun Dafa* is a modern *chi Kung* that produces a lot of energy in a simple way. I personally recommend the *Falun dafa* exercises, not the philosophical implications of this current of thought. If the negative emotions or feelings in your daily activity are too painful, heal them promptly according to the techniques explained in this book. Apply Gamma Energetics and release your cells. This increases the flow of *chi* or *prana* to enjoy the true pleasures of living in this physical body.

Be aware of your abdominal breathing in all activities. Make sure that you breathe with your abdomen. It doesn't matter if you look big-bellied; the important issue is the welfare you receive from this elementary practice, above the aesthetic appearance.

When opportunity comes to be outdoors on the field or the beach, try to meditate, practice yoga or do exercise. This is the sum of energy capturing. When you arrive home, be careful to select the type of information you want to receive as to not exhaust the remaining *chi* left in your body. The media must generate comforting, recreational and fun information to be able to disconnect ourselves from the issues that concern us daily.

In general, all activities that generate emotional pleasure like shows, concerts, art exhibitions, sporting events, music or dancing, increase the production of *prana* or *chi* in our bodies. Deep prayer, the intimate union with the divinity that provides abundant doses of universal love and benevolence, constitutes a powerful tool for Healing and therefore of energy gathering. When we humbly surrender to the infinite power of energy, we perceive the inner divinity imparted by Jesus and all the avatars that have passed through this level. This is reflected in a powerful charge of *prana* that rejuvenates and fortifies.

ILLUMINATION

I am this energy that comes forth from my heart.

I identify myself with the being that appears in my center-heart.

I am in unity of love with all things, animals and people.

I place the center of my mind in the heart- Chakra.

I am connected to Jesus (Buddha, Krishna, Rama, Zoroaster, Yahve, Ala).

I feel the infinite being within me.

I feel the ineffable happiness of being.

I feel the peace of the absolute present, without time.

I disconnect myself from low frequency thoughts, feelings, or emotions.

I harbor pure thoughts, feelings and emotions in my inner center.

Instead of being worried, my mind is concerned with being infinite in the now.

I find freedom in the center of my heart (heart-chakra).

I enjoy my inner quietness and peace.

My consciousness merges with the immensity of being.

I am this divine energy that comes from my heart

When negative thoughts appear I am in the false identity of the ego.

When I fall prey to negative emotions I live from the ego.

When I allow undesirable feelings to enter, I live in the ego, on the roller coaster of pleasure and pain.

I am conscious of my breathing method to break the circuit of thoughts and to be in the now.

With my breathing I tune in with the infinite being within me.

Through breathing I determine to always be in the frequency of the inner infinite being.

I am mindful of the happiness that emanates from within me.

Experience of the being, experience of being.

I breathe from my abdomen that inflates and deflates.

My consciousness is full of light, love and happiness.

The ego is my false identity.

I try to make decisions from the center-heart, from the being.

My decisions are full of universal love.

Being centered in my heart-chakra, I eliminate impulses and outbursts of character.

I remove all resentments from my psyche to live the present as a gift of life.

I perceive the vibration of love from others, being in the present.

All things, animals and people, are full of love.

When I am in the now I am a being full of pure love.

Love is the greatest force of the universes.

I give and receive love from others.

Friendship is the feeling of love for others.

I avoid responding to offenses. I send universal love to those who attack me.

My cells live in the love and compassion of the infinite being.

I am one with everything through love and compassion that arises when I am in the now.

Service to others gives me satisfaction and happiness.

I am kind, helpful and supportive of others.

A simple wish for bliss, balance and happiness to others is a great contribution of service.

I always perceive divinity in others, camouflaged in their ego.

Love and compassion that flow from being in the now fill me with unparalleled affection and bliss.

When I am within the infinite being, my actions are directed by pure love and compassion.

I believe in my true self that flows from the present-now, as a being of compassion, solidarity and love.

When I connect in the now with the infinite being, I eliminate suffering and pain.

From the now I erase fears, dangers and threats with my factual and transcendent self.

From the endless being within, death is a harmonious transition to eternal life of the infinite being.

Death is the cessation of the body to always live in the now, in the supreme bliss of being.

When I breathe I always remember to place my consciousness in the heart-chakra.

By acting from my spiritual heart I increase the frequency and vibration to reach the being.

I transmute all the energy I receive in love and compassion.

I purify my body and mind with the sublime energy that arises from my center-heart.

I always live in the present. I make fleeting visits to the past and the future while working.

I always send love and compassion to all that is.

I decree forever to always act from my heart, from my true identity, far from the ego.

I celebrate my awakening and ascension to live the now, from the infinite being.

I feel the divine grace within me.

I am a merciful being, connected to unity in love with all beings of all dimensions.

THE OASIS OF PEACE PYRAMID

With eyes closed and through the third eye or pineal gland, imagine a splendid room whose glass walls reflect a beauty of another dimension. The floor of this room is made of a shiny and translucent material resembling an immense mirror. When you take a few steps forward, you discover the three-dimensional image of Jesus Christ (Buddha, Ala, Moses, Krishna) who comes looking for you and gives you a huge hug that transports you to an unparalleled frequency where joy of the soul is ineffable.

As you advance a little more, you notice four large energy hollow-columns made of different chromatic tones. In front of you, a column of intense golden light. On your left, a column of red light. To your right is another column of Mediterranean blue light and behind you, one of intense green light.

As you go inside the golden column you are transported to times past where you used your magical abilities to heal others and direct the destinies of your life. You feel your body and your psyche being charged with energy, strength and power. An immense joy accompanies your passage through some of your past lives full of love and compassion. You experience the vigor and ability of the Excalibur sword in your dominant hand. The golden column symbolizes air as a vital element.

As you enter the red column, the different stages of your experiences in Atlantis arise. A whole body of esoteric knowledge that lies in your merkaba or body of light to be used in favor of others in healing and cleansing energy. You reaffirm your power as a universal Being and your ability to move in the different dimensions and planes of existence. Your connection with the divine from your center-heart is always present. This column represents fire as a vital element. The blue column reminds you of your experiences in Lemuria. Your contact with the sacred fire that helps to cleanse karma and facilitate your access to the earthly. You have experienced the energy of the glass libraries and their wonderful wave of divine light that brings you closer to truthfulness. In your body of light resides the most advanced scientific knowledge that you have absorbed in these incarnations. It is the water column.

The column behind you is green. For the purpose of creating the pyramid we will use its nutrient light for both your physical body and the other aspects that constitute your body of light. This column reflects your absolute present on earth and the modifications you can make in your psyche and therefore in your body and mind. Here you direct your transformation. This column symbolizes the land on which you live and dream. The planet that nourishes and sustains your bodies and psyche with energies.

Starting from the golden or air column, imagine a current of energy forming in an anti-clockwise direction that moves towards the red column, fire; continues towards the green column, earth; then to the blue column, water. Thus it continues its direction in an enveloping against-the-clock movement and going up the glass walls until arriving at the pyramidal dome, which is in the proportion of the great pyramid. Now begin your descent clockwise in a looping motion until you reach the base of the pyramid. The union of the four elements created the fifth element: pure love, ether, the fifth crystalline essence; the divine spirit. From the golden column the energy of pure love moves counterclockwise, upward through the glass walls and reaches the sumun of pure love in the dome of the pyramid. From there it is returned clockwise until it reaches the base of the pyramid. Now you can start the route from the red or fire column in an upwards wraparound direction, traversing all the elements: Fire, earth, water and air sheltered with the fifth element of pure and universal love.

From there it begins its downward spiraling journey in a clockwise direction until it reaches the base of the pyramid. You are in the center of the polyhedron, as an exceptional witness to the formation of the pyramid. You receive all the influence and information flowing within it. Now begin the journey from the green or earth column, traversing the water, air and fire gathered in the most powerful energy of the cosmos: pure and universal love. Return from the dome of the pyramid feeling the powerful force of pure love, as you go through all the glass walls and reach the base again.

You feel the influence of the most powerful motivation by the forcefulness of all the energies gathered there. Now start the route of your pyramid from the base in the water column in a counterclockwise upward spiral-pattern: air column (golden), fire column (red) and earth column (green). The most powerful love is then mobilized until you reach the dome of the glass pyramid. From there the love force moves clockwise towards the base with all the information accumulated and the intensity of the 5 elements that nourish you until you reach the marble floor.

Travel this path in two laps, starting again by the golden column to the left. When you have completed two laps, stay in the center of the pyramid and collect all the energies from all your lives and all the compounds that make up your bodies in order to feel the power and might of earth, air, water, fire and pure love. Sense how the pyramid fills with violet light that empowers and nourishes. Stay seated for 5 minutes, capturing all the energies and eliminating all the impurities of your bodies. Focus your mind on each of the four columns and then receive through the center of the pyramid a pillar of *Layoesh* light that beams down from the dome and invades all your bodies with blueish-white divine energy. After 2 minutes take a deep breath and leave the pyramid. Take at least five minutes to start with your activities.

You will now feel eternal peace within you. You will live under the shelter of angels and realize many situations in your life that lack depth.

You will find the path of contentment by living from the heart all the hardships and pains that become pure happiness in truthfulness or fifth dimension. You will understand that the pains belong to the mental world and perceive that when you transcend the absolute present, only blessings shall be received every day.

Practice this minimal meditation at least once a week and you will feel the calmness and happiness that comes from the high dimensions.

When you have problems, enter the pyramid and meditate on the 5 elements; thus you will find peace as a reward. *This is the abode of supreme Peace.*

Printed in the United States
By Bookmasters